Pinter's Son Jim

Pinter's Son Jim

an Australian Drama
by Henry Lawson

with "The Hero of Redclay"

Published by Bonfire Books,
753-755 Nicholson Street
Carlton North, VIC 3054, Australia
info@bonfirebooks.org
www.bonfirebooks.org

Manuscript completed 1897
First published 1984 in *A Camp-Fire Yarn* (Lansdowne)
First performed 1990 Combara, NSW by the Coonamble Theatrical Group
Preface © 2024 Lucas Smith

ALL RIGHTS RESERVED
No part of this publication may be reproduced, stored in a retrieval system, or transmitted in any form by any means electronic, mechanical, photocopying, recording or otherwise without the prior written consent of the publishers.

ISBN 978-0-6457768-5-0

A catalogue record for this book is available
from the National Library of Australia

Cover: detail from "Hill End Fantasy" (2022) by Ryan W Daffurn, collection of Chevalier Yves Hernot. Reproduced with permission.

Contents

Preface   7

Pinter's Son Jim

Act One   13

Act Two   56

Act Three   82

Act Four   98

Addendum: *The Hero of Redclay* 119

Preface

"TOO UNWIELDY TO STAGE". This is the verdict on *Pinter's Son Jim*.[1] Written in Wellington, New Zealand in 1897 while Lawson's wife was pregnant with their son (also "Jim"), the play was commissioned by theatre director Bland Holt, who then rejected it for production.

In truth, the chief difficulty of *Pinter's Son Jim* was probably not the number of required sets (including several domestic interiors, townscapes, river and desert wildernesses). Holt was accustomed to extravagance on stage, using a full circus in one play and being the first director to use a functional motor car in a theatrical production. The caving in of a creek bank, which occurs in *Pinter*, would not have been an issue for him. The much more likely real grounds for rejection is the contrived nature of the plot, which is overly reliant on coincidence, asides to the audience, eavesdropping and nick-of-time chance encounters. These continually pull the reader out of immersion in the story. The expository dialogue is not concealed well and probably would have sounded ham-handed in any age. Although Lawson's earlier fiction is intensely theatrical, consisting largely of dialogue and action, and a number of his stories have been made into short films, we must remember that this was his first and only foray into drama. As such it represents an untrodden path of tantalising possibility.

---

[1] Quote from Brian Mathews in his entry on Henry Lawson in the *Australian Dictionary of Biography*, but the sentiment is Holt's.

Lawson hoped that writing for the stage would make him wealthy, but for lovers of colonial Australian literature the loss is of a different nature. What Lawson as a fully developed dramatist may have achieved we will never know, but in *Pinter's Son Jim* there are hints: Mitchell's bawdy banter, the lampooning of the English "Colonial Experienced Man" and the ever-present weariness of outback life, which was Lawson's signature. These and many more parts of the play contain what makes Lawson an enduring figure.

The short story "The Hero of Redclay", included here as a gloss, is a much tighter, less melodramatic and decidedly gloomier version of the story of Jack Drew and Ruth Wilson of Cambaroora. The straight prose allows the full pathos of the tragic impasse between the two lovers to emerge in the reader's imagination, while the stage version drills it into your head, paradoxically lessening its power.

Lawson was probably still holding out hope for a theatrical career. In "Hero", published two years after *Pinter's Son Jim* was completed, the narrator "name-drops" the man who rejected the play. "The only well known man in Australia who reminds me of Mitchell is Bland Holt. Mitchell was about as good-hearted as Bland Holt, too, under it all..." After Mitchell tells him the "yarn" of *Pinter's Son*—a talented young man who drinks too much and takes the rap for someone else's crime for the sake of the honour of the girl he loves—the narrator reflects that the "story should have been played in the biggest theatre in the world, by the greatest actors, with music for intervals and situations—deep strong music, such as thrills and lifts a man from his boot soles."

The text is reproduced here exactly as it is set down in the first volume of the 1984 Lawson complete works, *A Camp-Fire Yarn*, edited by Leonard Cronin. The play was still in draft form. Lawson's notes for potential changes are retained and the missing manuscript page in Act Two is indicated. Lawson uses some American spellings e.g. 'Civilized' for 'Civilised' and these have been retained. There is some outmoded language, most notably the use of the word 'white', as in "She's rough but she's a white man underneath." White here meaning something like "honourable" or "upright", a man whose word can be trusted. *Pinter's Son Jim* was staged at least once, more than one hundred years after it was written, in 1990, by the Coonamble Theatrical Group, one of countless grassroots artistic organisations that keep arts and letters alive in regional Australia. This is its first publication as a stand-alone work[2]. We offer it to you as a respite from the cynicism of contemporary drama and as a tribute to Lawson's legacy.

Lucas Smith
March 2024

---

[2] To the best of our knowledge. If you are in possession of more details regarding the performance or publication history of this text, please contact us.

CAST OF CHARACTERS

Jack Drew—Editor *Cambaroora Star*: "clever but he drinks".
Doctor Lebinski—His friend, a Pole, a black sheep.
"Pinter"—An old mate of our father's.
Jim Poynton *(Pinter's son)*—A "wild colonial youth".
Jack Mitchell—A Bush Micawber.
J.B. Sawkins—Mining agent.
Brown—Bank manager at Cambaroora.
Mullaney—Constable at Cambaroora.
Cameron—Mounted trooper.
Bill Anderson *(otherwise the "Nipper")*—A Sydney newsboy.
Ruth Wilson—"A girl as God made her".
Mary—Partial to Mitchell.
Kate Kennedy—A Bush Girl who loved a scamp.
Bushmen, **Shearers** etc. etc.

Act One

Scene I

Township of Cambaroora. Dusty main street of typical country town in New South Wales. Mitchell painting round window of weatherboard cottage in foreground. Step ladder and small packing case to stand on. Paint pot, oil and turpentine cans, etc. Ragged blue gum tree in middle of street. Street running back to Royal Hotel in background.

MITCHELL: Well—what next I wonder? Cowboy on the farm; newsboy in the city; rag-and-bottle merchant; printer's devil; man-about-town—and here I am, stranded in the enterprising and boozy township of Cambaroora—a blooming artist in oils! The Jack of all trades in his time gets many times in the sack. *(Paints)* Graft is a mistake. It was all Adam's fault. If Adam had have let well alone, when he had a soft thing on, and not tried to find out things, there'd have been no graft in the world today. Trying to find out things is the cause of all the work and trouble in the world. Only for that there'd be no bloated capitalists, and no horny-handed working man, and no politics—no Freetrade and no Protection, and no clothes. The woman next door wouldn't be able to pick holes in your wife's washing on the line. We'd all be running about in a big Garden of Eden with nothing on and nothing to do except to loaf and make love, and lark and laugh, and play practical jokes on each other. That would be glorious—wouldn't it. *(Paints)* I'm going to chuck up graft—there's nothing in it—it's a fool's game. If I hadn't wasted my life working and looking for work; and getting the sack—and taking it—I'd have not been in this position today—I'd have been an independent man now. But I've made up my mind at last. I won't be a fool any longer—

I'm going to chuck up graft and go in for making money. *(Paints viciously. Mary, the housemaid, appears at window with a duster—starts to clean glass but draws back and watches Mitchell, unseen by him.)*

MITCHELL: *(Glancing over shoulder)* Here comes the vice-chairman of the Mudgee Budgee Funny Beggars. He'll want to try his hand, so I might as well have a brush ready for him. *(Paints, in abstracted manner, one side of broad flat handle of large "pound" brush thickly with sash tool in dark colour. Lays pound brush back across pot on ground—painted side of handle down—and goes on cutting in window frame in dark colour with sash tool.)* *(Enter Bush Larrikin—black glossy shop suit, etc. Swaggers up, surveys Mitchell and lifts his hat, grins, and pantomimes to Mary, who tosses her head, frowns and draws back)*

BUSH LARRIKIN: 'Ello, painter!

MITCHELL: Good-day, me fresh, sweet-scented beauty! *(Bush Larrikin swaggers—plants legs well apart—facing back of Mitchell's head)*

BUSH LARRIKIN: Say, painter!

MITCHELL: Say when.

BUSH LARRIKIN: You're putting it on wrong side out.

MITCHELL: *(Wearily—after glancing over wall)* It must be the weather that causes it.

BUSH LARRIKIN: Causes what? The paint to go wrong?

MITCHELL: No—you. *(Mary smiles gleefully. Bush Larrikin catches her eye and looks black)*

BUSH LARRIKIN: You think yourself pretty smart, don't you?

MITCHELL: Fairly so. Nothing to blow about. *(Goes on "laying off" colour on wall as lovingly as if his soul were in his work.)*

BUSH LARRIKIN: Say, painter?

MITCHELL: Say when. I'm ready.

Act I

BUSH LARRIKIN: Straight iron. No joke.

MITCHELL: Well, spit it out.

BUSH LARRIKIN: *(Pointing to painted weatherboard)* There's a bit fell off there.

MITCHELL: So it is. Perhaps you'd like to try your hand.

BUSH LARRIKIN: *(Airily)* Oh, I wouldn't mind having a shot at it. *(Swaggers to paint pot, takes up brush, sets it down hastily, and displays hand covered with dark paint)*

MITCHELL: Well, what'll I do next? I wonder? If I haven't gone and painted the handle of the brush I'm using. It must be the hot weather that makes us all a bit ratty. Would you mind scraping that off your hand into the pot? I'm short of colour.

BUSH LARRIKIN: *(Sees Mary laughing and gets mad)* You're smart, you are, but I'll take some of the smartness out of you in two acts when I start.

MITCHELL: Alright. Don't get anxious and worry yourself about it. What's your weapons? Swords or paint brushes? I'm the challenged party and—

BUSH LARRIKIN: I'll bloomin' quick show yer! You'll find me about when yer knock off. *(Softly for Mary's benefit)* I can use the bloomin' weppins that Nature giv' me.

MITCHELL: Alright, sonny—alright. But hadn't you better go and clean 'em up a bit first?

BUSH LARRIKIN: Clean up what?

MITCHELL: The weppins that Nature giv' yer.

BUSH LARRIKIN: *(Furiously)* I'll bloomin' quick show yer, when I start. *(Exit)*

MITCHELL: I wish he would start and show me something new. I'm tired of old things. *(Catches sight of Mary, winks at the audience, and after wiping the handle of the big brush, goes on painting—whistling the "Dead March" and moving brush to the tune) (Enter Jim Poynton. Leans against corner of painted wall, scratching the back of his head and watching Mitchell absently. Presently in an abstracted manner, he joins him in whistling "Dead March". This goes on for a while)*

MITCHELL: Sorry to trouble you, old man, but that paint's wet. *(Jim jerks shoulder from wall and stares at painted coat sleeve)*

MITCHELL: That's all right, mate. Don't apologise. I'll soon fix that. *("Lays off" smudged portion of wall carefully still whistling. Jim stares from the coat sleeve to Mitchell and back again, and scratches the back of his head)*

JIM: Well, I'm damned...Look here, painter, come and have a drink—you're a joker.

MITCHELL: Can't leave the job now. Thanks all the same.

JIM: Well I'll leave a beer in the bar at the Royal for you.

MITCHELL: Right you are.

(Exit Jim—into hotel)

MARY: *(At window)* Mr. Mitchell.

MITCHELL: Oh, it's Mary. Fresh as paint and sweet as mandarins! Well, what can I do for you, Mary?

MARY: Who told you that you could call me "Mary"?

MITCHELL: Instinct, Mary.

MARY: What nonsense, I don't know what you mean—I was just going to ask you if you'd like a cup of tea.

MITCHELL: I wish you would ask me, Mary.

MARY: Well, would you?

MITCHELL: If you please, Mary.

(Mary goes in. Mitchell winks broadly at the audience) That's the fifth cup of tea she's asked me if I'd like—not counting extras. I think it's good enough to do a bear up in that quarter. When a girl asks you twice if you'd like a cup of tea, it's a sign she likes you, when she asks you three times if you'd like a cup of tea, it's a sign she'd like to know whether you like her. *(Moves box into shaded angle of wall with his foot. Mary hands out cup of tea and plate of bread and butter)*

MITCHELL: Thank you, Mary. *(Mitchell settles himself comfortably on box. Mary starts cleaning window. Mitchell takes note and winks the other eye)*

MARY: *(Aside)* I wish he'd talk. *(To Mitchell)* You weren't always painting, Mr. Mitchell, were you?

MITCHELL: No, Mary, I should think not. I was in the rag-and-bottle line once.

MARY: Go away with you.

MITCHELL: *(Aside)* That means "come on".

MARY: But really—you weren't always a painter, were you? I heard that you were on a newspaper once with Mr. Drew, the editor of the *Star*.

MITCHELL: Well—look at that now. I *was* a journalist once, but I thought I'd lived that down. You might reform and live the past down in the city, but when you come to a bleak hole like this, you'll find your antecedents raked up against you. I've two minds to bring a libel action against this town. It's no use trying to reform. I'll give it best and drift back into literature again.

MARY: Oh! Don't do that!

MITCHELL: *(Aside)* There's more in her than I thought.

MARY: You know Mr. Drew?

MITCHELL: I should think so. He was under me once.

MARY: Under you, how?

MITCHELL: He was sub-editor on the old *Boomerang* in the city when I was the printers' devil.

MARY: What?

MITCHELL: No swearing, Mary. You don't know what the printers' devil is? Well, I'll tell you. He's the boy in the office. He's the first and final court of appeal on a newspaper. He's the chap that takes all the responsibility and kicks. He's the general manager, editor, fighting editor, sporting editor, religious editor, publisher, reporter, general advisor, detective, messenger, telephone boy, post-boy and scape-goat. Just as he's required. He's the one that invents on the spot and tells lies for the entire staff. He has to detect the spring poet, the man who wants to go into the sanctum and kick up a row, the constant reader who wants to drop in and have a chat with the editor for two or three hours on a busy day; and the pretty girl who wants to talk him into taking a little thing of her own. The devil has to detect them all and interview them first and if he can he has to circumvent them. He has to stow the valuable boozy member of the staff out of sight of the boss and pilot him home. He's the boy that has to know everything that's on the face of the earth and a good deal of underground engineering; and he's got to keep all this valuable information locked up in his bosom and tell lies instead and he's the first that has to go and root for himself when the paper goes bung.

MARY: You might as well keep all that locked up in what you call your bosom, for it's all Greek to me.

MITCHELL: I've got something locked up there that wouldn't be Greek to you, Mary.

MARY: And what's that?

MITCHELL: Woman's curiosity again.

MARY: Oh well. Keep it to yourself. I don't want to know.

MITCHELL: Alright, Mary—I'll tell you then. I think you're the jolliest, prettiest, best-hearted girl I've ever met—in the whole course of my career of course. *(Hands in cup)*

MARY: Oh, nonsense. Go along with your work and let me do mine.

MITCHELL: *(Standing back, brush in hand, and surveying his work critically)* Now, if I was a gentleman in independent circumstances, I'd buy that wall and send it to the Annual Art Society's Exhibition. It would make a more sensible picture than some I've seen there.

MARY: The idea! An old weatherboard wall daubed all over with what you call "stone colour"—and—and "salmon colour", and smelling like I don't know what.

MITCHELL: Yes, and a brand new girl in the window, with cheeks in what you call pink and white, and hair like Chinese

Act I

vermilion at a shilling a small packet, and eyes like—

MARY: Oh, do stop your nonsense. Is there any wet paint on this sill? *(Touches window sill gingerly)*

MITCHELL: No, I left it dry on purpose. *(Mary seats herself on window sill and starts cleaning outside glass. Mitchell shifts steps closer)*

MARY: Now then—you don't want the steps in the picture.

MITCHELL: Oh yes I do. Realistic touches are everything nowadays. Would you like to be in the picture, Mary?

MARY: Oh, nonsense.

MITCHELL: It couldn't look sweeter. *(Mary settles her dress and touches her hair and collar)* That picture would be snapped up by the National Art Gallery, and slated by the *Bulletin*, and cause no end of controversy in the newspapers.

MARY: Of what?

MITCHELL: *(Climbing steps)* Could I be in the picture too, Mary?

MARY: What nonsense! Who told you to come up here? Keep away. Go down or you'll paint me.

MITCHELL: You'll never want painting, Mary.

MARY: Go away.

MITCHELL: *(Aside)* That means "come on". *(Insinuating)* But couldn't I be in the picture too, Mary?

MARY: No. Why you'd crack the varnish and break the glass.

MITCHELL: I know I'm not a handsome chap, but—

MARY: Oh, I didn't mean that Ja—Mr Mitchell. I suppose you could be in it if you liked.

MITCHELL: Say "If you like, Jack".

MARY: Oh, nonsense.

MITCHELL: But just say it once, Mary.

MARY: Oh well. If—if you like, Ja—Jack. Now are you satisfied? What now—*(Mitchell puts his arm around her neck and kisses her)*

VOICE OF MISTRESS: Mary! *(Mary goes in with a jerk, bumping her head against the sash)*

MARY: You horrid animal. You've daubed me all over and your breath smells of beer enough to knock a person down! *(Slams down window sash)*

MITCHELL: There's another work of art gone wrong. *(Takes brush and paints to the accompaniment of "The Last Rose of Summer")* Well, it's about time they started the usual fight at the Nugget to give the respected townsmen of Cambaroora an excuse for their afternoon drink. It's wonderful how the male population gets caught in every dust-storm and hail-storm that comes along and has to seek shelter in the pubs.

(Commotion about the Nugget Hotel. Loafers rush inside) Speak of the devil!

(Shouts) Fight-ho!

(Male population of Cambaroora rushes across stage and from doors, and into the Nugget Hotel followed by Mitchell. Great row heard going on at the Nugget)

(Enter from hotel: Jim Poynton, Sawkins, Mitchell, Pinter, Kate Kennedy and excited crowd of shearers, loafers, etc.)

CROWD: I'll back you, Jim!

JIM: Come on, boys. We'll go down to the river bank and have it out.

SAWKINS: I won't lower myself to fight you. But I'll have satisfaction. What sort of a town is this where a gentleman can't go into an hotel without being assaulted by a blackguard? Where is the constable?

KATE: Don't you dare call Jim a blackguard. Who are you and what are you? There's plenty of gentlemen of your sort come here.

JIM: Hold your tongue, Kate, and go back to the bar. I'll settle him.

KATE: I won't.

JIM: *(To Sawkins)* Put up your hands.

Act I

Shearer: Hold on, Jim. Here's Mullaney.
(Enter Constable Mullaney)
MULLANEY: Phwats this, lads? What's the meanin' o' this? Can't Oi turn me back for aminit, but ye must turn the town upside down for a couple of hours. Oi'll make an example of every man of ye.

VOICE: It's Pinter's son Jim.

MULLANEY: An' who towld ye to turn Queen's evidence? Oi know it's Pinter's son Jim. It's always Pinter's son Jim. Now what have you got to say for yourself, Jim?

JIM: There was a pack of card sharpers and spoilers swindling a mug in the bar parlour and Dad spotted one of them faking the cards. The old ass put his oar in and three or four of them mobbed him. And I come in.

MULLANEY: And who's the sharpers yer talking about? Be careful what ye say, Jim.

MITCHELL: One of them's laid up for repair and the rest smoked.

MULLANEY: And is that arl?

SAWKINS: No, I give that man *(pointing to Jim)* in charge, for assault and battery.

MITCHELL: It's alright, Jim. I'll bail you out.

MULLANEY: Yes, and swear him out afterwards. Howld your tongues. What's you name, sir?

SAWKINS: J.B. Sawkins. Mining and Commission Agent. *(Gives card)* I had joined in a game of cards with two men who are strangers to me, and was endeavouring to make peace when the man you call Pinter and his gang started the row. That man struck me. *(Pointing to Jim)*

JIM: Strangers to you? Why you're hand in glove with them. They're a damned push, Mullaney.

MULLANEY: Howl dyer tongue, Jim, be careful what you say. Where's your father? Where's Pinter?

CROWD: Liza the cook is holding him down, sitting on him.

MULLANEY: The saints defend him. She's eighteen stone if she's an ounce. She'll be committing matrimony wid him next. Go and rescue the man, some of yez. Ye'd better take out a summons Mr. Sawkins.

SAWKINS: Did you hear, Constable? I give that man in charge. Am I to understand that you refuse to do your duty?

MULLANEY: Ye'll find Oi'll do my duty, Mr. Sawkins—or whoever ye are.

SAWKINS: I'll report you.

MULLANEY: Take care my report isn't in lasht.

(Enter Jack Drew)

JACK: It's alright, Mullaney. I know Mr Sawkins. He'll let the matter drop.

SAWKINS: *(Startled)* I don't know you, and I don't want to. I'll take out a summons, Constable.

(Exit Sawkins)

MULLANEY: He seems not to know ye, Drew.

JACK: He ought to. Look here, Mullaney. There's a push in this town that ought to be cleared out.

MULLANEY: Thin give the bhoys the hint then. Oi've got enough to do to keep the blaggards in order themselves—what wid their unionism and brotherhood an' drinkin', an' gamblin', an' foightin' won another, al' larkin' an' bilin' wan another out, an' swearin' wan another off—an' fright'nin' witnesses. Oi don't care how soon shearin' starts agin. Oi must go to the Nugget and see about this gamblin'.

SHEARER: There's a drink in the bar for you, Constable.

MULLANEY: Never yez moind. Ye're all mighty good to Mullaney when ye're got some devilment on. Oi can get me own dhrinks whin Oi want them, without troublin' yez.

(Goes to pub)

SHEARER: Go on, Kate, and draw him a long one.

(Kate follows Mullaney)

JACK: Look here, you chaps. I want a few words with you.

Act I

SHEARER: Right you are Jack—fire away!

JACK: We've got a hard enough life as it is in this God-forsaken part of the country. Lord knows we throw away our money quickly enough when we get it without being swindled out of it by gangs of paltry sharpers.

SHEARER: Hear, hear. Now the bushman can't come into town and have his spree without a gang of city spoilers and bummers loafing on him for drinks, cheating him at cards when he's muddled. Shepherding him every hour in the day, sneaking after him in the dark and robbing him when he's drunk—the crawlers are not above knocking a man down from behind when they get a chance. There's a push of that sort in town now. It doesn't pay the publican to take action, and Mullaney is one man.

SHEARER: We'll take action!

JACK: In my father's time such crawlers would have been given one hour to clear out of town.

SHEARER: We'll give 'em less. That's alright, Jack—we'll fix it. Now, chaps, three cheers for Jack Drew and the *Cambaroora Star*.

SHEARERS: Hip, hip, hoorah! Etc. Come on Jack and wet yer air pipe after that.

(Enter Mullaney)

MULLANEY: And Oi'll jist give yer arl two second start to disperse. An' if there's a whisper of a row in the town tonight Oi'll fix up a nice little charge for every wan of ye that'll keep ye going till next shearing. Be arf now, an' stop shpitting and shplathering arl over the tow path.

(Exit crowd, laughing, to pub)

CROWD: Come along, Mullaney.

MULLANEY: Ah well. The saints deliver me. Oi suppose Oi'll have to go an' look after thim. *(Follows crowd into pub)*

MITCHELL: There's Jack Drew—up at the pub again. It's a blooming pity. He came up here to straighten up too—and now he's in it again. It's a blooming pity. The best thing he could do would be to take me with him again. *(Slaps brush against wall disconsolately)* He's about the whitest and straightest man I've met yet in the whole course of my chequered career—and the cleverest pen of 'em all—he could write rings around 'em all. It's a blooming pity. I dunno how it is. The best and cleverest and whitest men in this country seem to take to drink mostly. Perhaps it's because they're straight and the world's crooked. And poor Jack Drew. It's a thundering jumped up pity. *(Paints to the tune of "Bonnie Dundee")*

(Enter Mullaney—wiping his mouth—and with a broad smile on his face. Crosses his legs, facing audience, and at the same time supports himself with hand against corner of painted house. Takes hand away suddenly, covered with paint)

MULLANEY: Phwat's this? What do you mane by this?

MITCHELL: What's the matter, Constable?

MULLANEY: Phwat's the matter? Look at me hand. Whoy don't ye wroit up whit paint acrost it?

MITCHELL: There's "Wet Paint" chalked on the ground.

MULLANEY: Well. Oi don't read with me feet, do Oi?

MITCHELL: Well I can't help it. If I write up "wet paint", every fool touches it to see if it's dry. And if I write up "dry paint", they'd want to see if it was wet. *(Goes on repairing damage with brush)*

MULLANEY: Ye'd best be careful young man, or Oi'll fix up a nice little charge for ye that'll put ye where ye won't see anything but dry whitewash for a month.

MITCHELL: Why, what have I done.

MULLANEY: What have ye done? What haven't ye done? Puttin' the boys up to arl sorts of devilment wid the yarns of the sprees ye had in the city, an' the New Year's Nights, an' arl that. Oi've got me eye on ye. Move on an' get on wid ye're worruk!

Act I

(*Exit Mullaney*)
(*Mitchell paints to the tune of "Kathleen Maroon"*)
(*Enter Jack Drew from The Nugget, rather the worse for liquor*)

JACK: Hello, Mitchell! That tune won't pay.

MITCHELL: It'll pay me, Mr Drew. I'm on day work. Lovely tunes play a man out of a pub too soon in this country.

JACK: Who's Mr Drew? I'm Jack still to you, Mitchell. *(Hold out his hand)*

MITCHELL: And I'm Mitchell—still on the move.

JACK: Well, how have you been getting on since the old *Boomerang* shed? Do you like painting rather than newspaper office work?

MITCHELL: It's honester, anyway, and there's less anxiety about it. You see, a printer's devil is alright so long as he has an editor and staff under him that he can trust. But when the editor goes in for what he calls straight honest journalism, and gets a libel action on the paper, and gets run in, and the ghost vanishes, and the plant is seized for debt, it's cruel rough on the devil.

JACK: Oh well, let the old ghost of the old *Boomerang* rest, Mitchell. We made a good fight for it, and died hard.

MITCHELL: Yes, I reckon some of us haven't forgotten the last issue or two yet. But the *Boomerang* knocked me into the street, selling opposition papers.

JACK: By the way, what do you think of Mary, the housemaid, Mitchell? I notice you go in for tea and bread and butter lately.

MITCHELL: Do you? That reminds me, by the way, I notice you go in for a cup of cocoa and cake sometimes.

JACK: *(Aside—and a bit staggered)* That serves me right. What do you know about that Mitchell?

MITCHELL: Your office window opens on the back yard doesn't it?

JACK: Well?

MITCHELL: There was a bit of painting going on at the new stables at the back the other morning.

JACK: Well?

MITCHELL: And a cup of cocoa and some sheep's eyes crossed each other over the fence.

JACK: You kept very close.

MITCHELL: Well, that's what I'd like a mate of mine to do, if I had a little affair on hand.

JACK: That will do, Mitchell. She's a good true girl and it isn't right for us to talk about her like this.

MITCHELL: *(Reflectively addressing painted wall)* I knew a chap once—a sort of chum of mine—a chap clever enough to rise to any position. He took to drink and was going to the dogs when he met a girl, like—like Miss Wilson, for instance. He married her, and reformed and went up to the top of the tree. *(Jack rests his elbow on the steps and his head on his hand. Mitchell whistles a bar or two of "Annie Laurie")*

MITCHELL: Say, Jack! I was down fishing in the bend of the creek the other morning and Miss Wilson came along.

JACK: Well, what did she say?

MITCHELL: She said "Good evening."

JACK: Well?

MITCHELL: I said, "Good evening, miss." Somehow or other I hadn't the cheek to talk to her like I'd like to—to—

JACK: Mary, for instance.

MITCHELL: Never you mind. There's some girls that a vagabond chap can't talk to like he'd talk to other girls. She asked me if I'd caught any fish and I said, "No, miss." She asked me if it wasn't me down there fishing with Mr Drew the other evening, and I said, "No, miss," you were out of town. I asked her if she'd like to have a try with my line, but she said, "No thanks, I must be going." Then she said, "Good evening," and started off along the bank all alone by her sweet self.

JACK: Well, what does all this come to?

MITCHELL: *(Painting carefully)* Oh! Nothing! Only I was thinking, Jack, that if you'd been there, she'd have stayed and she might have caught a fish.

JACK: Look here, Mitchell. If you don't shut up I'll knock some of the devilment out of you.

MITCHELL: You're too straight for a journalist, Jack.

JACK: Indeed. Thank you for the compliment.

MITCHELL: Yes, you should have been a lawyer.

MARY: *(Suddenly appearing at the window)* Jack! There's your boss down the street. *(Sees Drew and bobs back. Mitchell paints to the tune of "Bonnie Dundee")*

(Boss comes past casually, and looks at watch)

BOSS: That wall looks alright, Mitchell, you can knock off when you get round that bit of wall at the corner.

MITCHELL: Right you are, sir.

(Boss goes into pub)

That's the way of it—you can knock off when you've done a couple of square miles.

JACK: Look here, Mitchell. If you feel that way I'd find room for you on the *Star*. I want a devil I can trust to look after the paper, and I'll do what I can for you.

MITCHELL: *(Holding out his hand)* It's a bargain. Say when.

JACK: *(Shaking hands)* Whenever you're ready.

MITCHELL: Right-ho. Monday morning. I've got to give the finishing touches to this work of art first.

(Jack starts towards pub)

He's going up to the trough again. I can run the *Star*, but I don't know about the other devil that's got him. *(Slaps brush on wall)* There's going to be a literary boom in Cambaroora if I get a free hand.

(Enter Pinter. The worse for liquor)

And there's old Pinter now. He's on the booze, but he'll come off if he thinks Jack is going on. He always does, they say.

PINTER: 'Ullo, Jack Drew. Here's an old mate o' your father's. Where yer off ter?

JACK: Where you came from, The Nugget. Come along, old party.

PINTER: *(Pulling himself together and looking at Jack Drew)* Yer agoin' on the spree again. Don't say a word—I can see it in yer eyes.. Stop where yer are!

JACK: Nonsense, Pinter, you're boozed.

PINTER: Jack Drew. I was an ole mate o' yer father's.

JACK: I know you were, Pinter, and a very good mate too.

PINTER: Stop where yer are. I'm goin' back for a soda; an' if I catches yer anigh a pub tonight—or makin' a fool o' yerself—I'll make a roley show o' yer! Stop where yer are. I'm an ole mate o' yer father's.

(Goes back to pub)

JACK: Pinter thinks I'm going on the bust. I shouldn't wonder but the old ass has gone to hunt up Doctor Lebinski. Well, I've got to have a drink anyway—If I go to the Halfway House for it.

(Starts for pub and meets Doctor Lebinski entering)

DOCTOR: Ello, Jack! Where are you running to?

JACK: The office. Where are you running to?

(Doctor takes Jack by the arm and leads him down front)

JACK: I've just been comparing notes with an old printer's devil of ours on the old *Boomerang*. I've taken him on again.

DOCTOR: *(Looking Jack in the eyes)* You've just been comparing notes with another old devil of ours, from the old Garden of Eden, and you're taking him on again. I want to talk to you.

JACK: Oh bosh! Don't preach! *(Recklessly)* I must have a whisky and soda for my nerves. Come and have a drink and then you can talk till all's blue.

DOCTOR: Just so! Come and have a drink at the creek. The

walk will do you good and I'll give you something for your nerves afterwards. I've got something to say to you. Come along.

(Takes him off)

MITCHELL: That's better. I'll back an old boozer that's been through it all and knows to save a young one before all the parsons and cold tea he-males in the world.

(Exit with steps, pot and brush)

(Enter Brown and Sawkins)

BROWN: Well, do you think we'll pull it through alright?

SAWKINS: Of course we will. Trust me. The name of the field is a gold mine in itself. I showed you the prospectus.

BROWN: Yes, you had to stretch your imagination a bit.

SAWKINS: I'll stand the strain. Well, we've got enough money in the city to pay expenses, and something over. And as soon as Pinter bottoms the shaft on payable gold we'll float this company and sell—or sell first as things work out. When did Pinter say he expected to finish the shaft?

BROWN: Tomorrow, I want cash at once, and so do you, I suppose.

SAWKINS: N.S.F. at the bank I suppose.

SAWKINS: Oh, nothing as usual. *(Aside)* Something wrong with his cash, I must make a note of that.

Come now, don't let us be fools, Brown , we know each other too well to quarrel. When do you want the cash?

BROWN: I want it before the seventeenth of next month at the latest.

SAWKINS: *(Aside)* That settles it. He expects his inspector about the seventeenth. That'll be alright I think. We're sure to pull off one of the little specs we've got on hand.

BROWN: But suppose Pinter doesn't bottom on payable dirt.

SAWKINS: Leave that to me. He'll strike the richest lead ever found in Cambaroora. We'll have to square him, that's all.

BROWN: Square him? How'd you mean?

SAWKINS: Gammon, you don't know. Put salt on an old bird's tail.

BROWN: Salt the claim, eh! Well, well you needn't have told me that.

SAWKINS: Quite unnecessary, I know.

BROWN: The streets have ears. Best keep those sort of things to yourself.

SAWKINS: Alright, I will. *(Aside)* And other things too. The question is: can we square Pinter?

BROWN: We'll have to let him stand in, that's all. He's only been working for bare-living wages for us, you know, and I know he's pushed for want of money just now.

SAWKINS: But he's straight isn't he?

BROWN: As straight as the rest of us when the pinch comes. If he tries any of his nonsense I know how to fix him.

SAWKINS: Got a hold on him, eh? Well, that's alright. We might as well go and look him up now.

BROWN: But you forget. I've got nothing to do with it, remember? I'm not in.

SAWKINS: Well the sleeping partner might have to talk in his sleep. But that's all right. Trust me—you're only a friend of mine. Come along.

(Exit Brown and Sawkins)
(Enter Doctor Lebinski and Jack Drew)

DOCTOR: Yes, Ruth is a girl as God made her. There are too few like her in this world. Poor girl, she has had a hard life for one so young since her father died. You met him once, you said.

JACK: Yes, and I have cause to remember his name with gratitude. He helped me out of a hole; and I almost a total stranger to him.

DOCTOR: That was like Wilson. When Ruth's mother

died—I knew Ruth's mother before she married Wilson, before she came to this country, we were boy and girl at school together, at home in Poland. But that's my story—the story of my life. When Ruth's mother died the girl was adopted by an aunt or, rather, her mother's half-sister, the wife of Brown, the bank manager here.

JACK: I know that, Ruth told me so.

DOCTOR: And perhaps you have an idea what such self-sacrificing family kindness generally means. The girl was made to work like a slavey; snubbed, and treated with contempt by even the youngest spoilt brat in the family. Taunted with her dependence, and the alleged kindness of her relations thrown up to her, one way or another, every hour in the day. It's a cruel position for any girl, and doubly cruel for a girl like Ruth.

JACK: If I had known that—

DOCTOR: What would you have done? *(Jack bows his head and is silent)* Her life here is a lonely one. She is not liked by other girls. She will never be popular with women, because she is too true. She is so fond of speaking the truth which a pure life has set in her eyes. She likes you for the better side of your nature, which a woman's instinct shows her. You are the only one here, except perhaps me, who seems to understand, or be in sympathy with her. She is grateful for the little kindness you have done her; and Jack, she pities you. You know what that leads to with a woman.

JACK: And me—God help me! I love her.

DOCTOR: God help Ruth, for she loves you.

JACK: How do you know that?

DOCTOR: I know it. Twenty years of regret have taught me to see things. Ruth is a girl who only loves once, but it means her whole life.

JACK: She is too good for this place. She is too good for this world.

DOCTOR: She is too good for this man. But the harm is

done now. Is she good enough for a careless man—whose own carelessness had led her on to love him? Is she good enough for him to reform—to be a man—for her sake? Jack, she is too pure to understand the vileness of this world. You are seen with her often. She is not popular with the hags here—you know what their tongues are like in a local hole like this. Now, listen to me. I know you better than you know yourself. I know that you are, at heart, a better man than the average. But I have loved Ruth as a daughter, ever since I first held her in my arms—a laughing baby girl, and, if I were sure that you would go on drinking and wasting your life, as you are doing now, I would rather see her dead than tied to you. Now listen. There are only two courses open to you: either marry her and rejoice, or sell your paper and go right away from here for her sake. You'll most likely break her heart in any case, but you must decide now.

JACK: Doctor, you should have been a good husband and father.

DOCTOR: I might have been.

JACK: But Doc, you are not an old man. Is—was there no woman?

DOCTOR: Yes, she is in heaven. Listen, Jack, twenty years ago there was a careless young vagabond like you going to the dogs as you are now, and there was a girl—a girl like Ruth—that tried to save him—

JACK: *(Laying his hand on the Doctor's shoulder)* Doc, old man, I'm sorry. I'm sorry that I touched that old wound.

DOCTOR: Never mind that, Jack. I have had my chances and taken them or missed them, as my story goes. I have lived my life and must be satisfied. You have yours before you.

JACK: I will fight it out tonight and tell you in the morning. *(They shake hands)*

DOCTOR: If you do not, it will mean many a bitter, unavoiding, midnight fight for you in years to come.

Act I

(Exit Doctor Lebinski)

JACK: *(After pacing up and down)* It is no use. I know myself too well. I have fought it out and reformed too often. The vagabond blood is too strong in my heart and the damned taste for drink is inherited from generations. If my childhood and boyhood had been a happy one—but this is cowardice. I have only myself to blame. Why take a night to think over it? If I took a year it would be the same. How could I ask a good, true girl to link her life to that of a vagabond like I am? It would be a hell for her, and, my God, a hell for me. She will forget. She will forget. Better the short, sharp pain than a life of lingering misery, of cruel misery for her. I will at least not have that on my soul in the end. In the end—a bar-room loafer—a dirty drunkard's death.

(Ruth enters, and stands watching Jack)

The devil of unrest is in me again. I must have a drink, I must drink tonight, and tomorrow I will sell the *Star* and go—for Ruth's sake.

(Starts towards hotel and meets Ruth)

JACK: Good evening, Miss Wilson.

RUTH: Good evening, Mr Drew. *(Awkward pause)*

JACK: I—I—Are you going for a stroll, Miss Wilson? *(Aside)* She must think I've been drinking.

RUTH: Yes, I thought I would like a walk by the creek, in the cool of the afternoon. Hasn't it been terribly hot today?

JACK: Yes—that is—yes it has. *(Aside)* I feel hotter now.

RUTH: I suppose you are going to the office, Mr Drew.

JACK: Yes I was. But now I think I'd like a breath of fresh air too. Would you like me to come, I mean, would you have any objections to my accompanying you, Miss Wilson? *(Aside)* That last drink's gone to my head.

RUTH: Oh no, not at all. I'd be so glad if you—I mean I'm rather nervous, going out by myself with all those swagmen camped about the town. *(Aside)* Oh! He must think me a little fool!

JACK: You need never fear an insult from a real Australian bushman, Miss Wilson. That is, I mean, when I am—after all, it is not wise to wander around the bush alone. *(Aside)* Damn it! I'll put both feet in it before I'm done.

(Exit Ruth and Jack)

(Doctor Lebinski crosses stage, raising his hat as he passes)

(Mitchell brings steps round, plants them on stage, climbs up and looks after Ruth and Jack. Gets down and waltzes round with steps, whistling "Annie Laurie". Mary appears at window)

MITCHELL: Say, Mary, I think I'll take my fishing rod and go down to the creek this evening.

MARY: Will you? Well, what's that got to do with me?

MITCHELL: Do you think I'll catch anything, Mary?

MARY: What a nonsensical question. You won't catch one anyway. *(Closes window)*

MITCHELL: *(Solus)* I'll chance it anyway. I might get a bite.

(Exit with steps)

(Enter Brown, Sawkins and Pinter. Pinter very much excited)

SAWKINS: Will you be quiet, you fool? You're drunk.

BROWN: Come to my office. We can't discuss business in the street.

PINTER: Street or no street, I'll say what I have to say. We said what we had to say in the streets in the old days. We lived in tents in them days and our offices was there. If damned scoundrels wanted to work a swindle they went into the bush to do it—and it wasn't always safe then.

BROWN: Have a care. Be careful. Do you know who you are talking to?

PINTER: Yes, I know you. You paid me to put down a prospecting shaft and I done it. And now you ask me—*me*, Old Pinter of old Ballarat and Bendigo—me that lived through the Roarin' Days—me that was mates with men like Drew—Jack Drew's father—asked by a pair of damned scoundrels to salt a claim and tell Jack Drew a lying yarn to put in his paper—to swindle jackaroos and new chums. I'll see you both in blazes first for a pair of—!

BROWN: Stop that, Pinter, or you'll regret it. No one spoke of salting a claim. Now listen to me. I know your son Jim. Only your name and money—and the influence of Jack Drew and one or two others has kept him out of gaol so long. Now, I know enough to put him where all the gold found on Ballarat or Bendigo in "them days" as you call them, wouldn't get him out for many a long day to come.

PINTER: You cowardly cur! If I only had a witness. There was no witnesses expected in them days—it was man to man; and no white man's word stood on me.

BROWN: Never mind witnesses or your son Jim will have more than he wants. Now, look here—Sawkins will pay you the balance of your wages in coarse Cambaroora gold. When you bottom that shaft tomorrow, you'll bottom on good gold—you'll strike a rich lead, and report the fact to Drew in time for the next issue of the *Star*—or Jim goes to gaol!

MITCHELL: *(Suddenly appearing, brush in hand, from behind the corner of painted house)* Not if I know it. Declined with thanks. Send stamps for return of manuscript!

SAWKINS & BROWN: Who the devil are you?

MITCHELL: The printers' devil on the old *Boomerang*, Jack Mitchell. Mr John Mitchell, new associate editor of the *Cambaroora Star*. I know you, Sawkins, alias half-a-dozen other names—you've picked out a pretty one this time. You remember the *Boomerang*? We stopped one of your little games once.

Scene II

Cambaroora Road near town. Enter Kate and Jim Poynton.

KATE: You'll get into trouble over this, Jim. One of those jackaroos has taken out a summons, and that's what I came out to tell you.

JIM: Who is it?

KATE: That fellow named Sawkins, I think.

JIM: How do you know?

KATE: Constable Mullaney and Constable Cameron were talking about it in the bar.

JIM: While you were there?

KATE: Yes, I think Mullaney wanted me to hear and give you the tip. He's got a sneaking kind of a liking for you, Jim, I think. He said that the best thing you could do would be to clear out and stay away for a while; and I think so too, Jim. You're doing no good here—you know that, Jim. Go Out Back, get a job and pull yourself together, for—for your father's sake, if you don't do it for mine. I believe it's only on your account that he's drinking now.

JIM: Kate, you're a trump! *(kisses her)* I will, I'll turn over a new leaf now. Cheer up, Kitty, I mean it this time! I'll go Out Back and work out my own salvation one way or the other. I won't be a damned fool any longer. And you must forget me, Kate—or at least till I come back a different sort of chap.

KATE: I sometimes wish I could forget you, Jim. But I—I can't.

JIM: Come, now, don't fret Kate. Keep on remembering me. You've got my word now, and may God strike me dead if I forget it. I'll go tonight.

KATE: But have you got any money, Jim?

JIM: That's alright.

KATE: But I know you're hard up. Look, Jim, I've saved five pounds. I don't want it, and besides you can send it back when you've made a cheque. Take it to please me.

JIM: No, Kate, I won't. I'll manage alright.

KATE: Here's someone coming, and I must hurry back. Here take the money, Jim, don't be foolish.

JIM: *(Taking her in his arms and kissing her)* No, Kate, I'm not so low as that. Cheer up, don't cry, Kate, for God's sake.

KATE: *(Raising her head from his shoulder)* Good—good-bye, Jim.

JIM: Good-bye, Kate. *(Another kiss and she runs off crying)*
(Enter Ruth and Jack Drew. Jim lifts his hat and looks at Jack as they pass)

JACK: Excuse me for a moment, Miss Wilson. That is Pinter's son Jim. I think he wanted to speak to me.

RUTH: Certainly.

(Jack turns back to Jim)

JACK: Well. Jim, anything new?

JIM: I've got to clear off. I wanted to say good-bye. That was all.

JACK: Is it as bad as that? When are you off?

JIM: Now—tonight.

JACK: Well, Jim, I wish you luck. Get something steady to do, and settle down for the old man's sake. Chuck up booze and cards, Jim, there's nothing in it—take my tip. I'm going to do it.

JIM: Same here. *(Holding out hand)* Good-bye, Jack, and god bless you.

JACK: Good-bye, Jim, old man, keep a stiff upper lip. By the way—how are you fixed? Are you stiff?

JIM: I'll battle alright.

JACK: Nonsense, old man. *(Glances towards Ruth)* Lend me your tobacco pouch. *(Jim hands out pouch. Jack ostentatiously fills his pipe from it and slips in some pound notes, and hands pouch back)*

Both: Good-bye, old man.

(Exit Jack and Ruth)

JIM: *(Opening pouch and transferring notes to pocket)* And if anybody ever has a word to say against Jack Drew, I only hope I'll be there when he says it, to knock the crawler down; and if ever Jack Drew gets into a hole, I only hope that I'll be there to help him out. For Jack Drew is a white man!

Scene III

On the bank of She-Oak Creek. Mitchell and Mary sitting close together on the bank. Mitchell fishing—with one arm round Mary's waist.

MITCHELL: *(Aside)* I thought I'd get a bite.
MARY: I'll tell you a secret, Jack.
MITCHELL: Alright, Mary. *(Aside)* That will be something new for a woman.
MARY: You know Ruth Wilson, the girl at the bank?
MITCHELL: I've seen her.
MARY: Do you like her?
MITCHELL: I like what I've seen of her.
MARY: I think she's the dearest, best and truest girl I've ever met.
MITCHELL: I don't think so.
MARY: Why?
MITCHELL: Because you're here.
MARY: Oh, nonsense. Well, I was telling you, all the chaps in Cambaroora are mad after her.
MITCHELL: I ain't. I'm ratty after someone else.
MARY: Never mind that. She wouldn't look at one of them and I don't blame her.
MITCHELL: It would be different if she looked at 'em all.
MARY: She could look at you as much as she liked for all I'd care. Never mind, you know Mr Drew?
MITCHELL: I've heard of him.
MARY: Well, he's Mr Right.
MITCHELL: Oh, is he? *(Aside)* I'll hear something new some day.
MARY: It's such a pity he drinks.
MITCHELL: Why he'd die of thirst if he didn't.
MARY: You know what I mean. It's a pity he drinks spirits.

MITCHELL: Yes, that stuff they sell here. I prefer bottled ale. But there's two things in the world that might make a teetotaller of a man when everything else fails.

MARY: And what are they, pray?

MITCHELL: One's matrimony, and the other the gallows.

MARY: *(Rising)* You horrid animal! I'll never speak to you again!

MITCHELL: *(Jumping up)* Keep quiet, I've got a bite.

MARY: Mind you don't fall in, Jack, that bank's slippery.

(Bank gives way and Mitchell falls in)

MARY: There, I told you so. Oh! Help! Help! Swim out, Jack. Here *(holding out rod)* catch hold of the end of the rod.

MITCHELL: *(Clinging to stump in water)* Hold on! Don't pull! The hook's caught in my pants!

MARY: Come out at once. What are you doing?

MITCHELL: Taking my clothes off.

MARY: What? Come out at once. You ought to be ashamed of yourself. Come out, Jack. You can swim in your clothes.

MITCHELL: But you don't want me to come out wringing wet do you?

MARY: Oh Jack. *Do* come out.

MITCHELL: I wanted to see whether I'm born to be drowned. *(Climbing out)* I'm born to be hung. *(On the bank, the hook caught in the seat of his pants)* You've caught me, Mary.

MARY: Yes and a nice fish you are. Look at yourself. Go straight home and change or you'll get your death of cold. *(She still has the rod in her hands)*

MITCHELL: Well, now you've landed me you might as well take the hook out of my gills.

MARY: Take it out, be quick, there's a storm coming. *(Lightning and thunder)* We'll get wet.

MITCHELL: I can't get any wetter.

MARY: Come away quick, Jack. There's somebody coming.

(Moves off with rod)

MITCHELL: She's got a bite.

(Enter Ruth Wilson and Jack Drew)

JACK: Well, that's the story of my life, Miss Wilson. The story of a careless, vagabond, mistaken life at the best, and a strange story for a man to tell a girl. I don't know why I told you—except that you have a good, true, and sympathetic heart—and the hardest, bitterest men crave for sympathy at times. All I know is that I feel better for telling you. Perhaps, when I am gone, one at least will think of me—not as the man I am but as the man I might have been.

RUTH: I always will—and as the man you really are—your true self. I am glad you told me what you have. I do not know why, but I feel glad of it. You have been wronged, and you have suffered, but that is past. Let it be past. Do not brood over old wrongs—real and fancied wrongs, and wasted opportunities. You are young—you have your whole life before you. You are clever. Why waste your time in a place like this? Why not write a book? Why not write the story of your own life? You have the ability—the genius—and it might win you both fame and fortune. I feel sure that it would.

JACK: I will, some day.

RUTH: Some day! That word is the key note of the lives of thousands of failures. *Now* is the word. Start *now*, today, tonight! Never put it off! And another thing, Mr Drew, you must not be angry with me for saying this. It is strange, I know, for a girl like me to talk to a man in this way, but I was always looked upon as a strange girl, and—

JACK: I don't think so.

RUTH: I have had a hard life, too, and learnt many things beyond my age. I feel that I am right in speaking to you now. Mr Drew, could you not leave drink alone? It does you no good. You lose the respect of your best friends, and above all your own self-respect. Don't be offended or angry with me.

JACK: *(Gently)* I would never be that—

RUTH: But—but leave the drink alone if only for my sake *(Aside)* Oh! What have I said to him now? *(Bows her face in confusion.)*

JACK: *(After a struggle with himself)* Ruth! Ruth! I cannot help it, for I love you, Ruth. I meant to go away without telling you this, but cannot. You like me, I know, or you pity me. Could you—could you—have sufficient faith in one to believe that I *will* reform for your sake—to trust your future with me? Ruth, could you love me and trust me enough to be my wife?

RUTH: I have that faith. I do trust you. And I—

JACK: *(Taking her in his arms)* And you—Ruth?

RUTH: Will be your wife. *(Vivid flash of lightning, clap of thunder. Ruth clings to Jack, who draws her under shelter of a tree and puts his overcoat around her)*

(This scene continued or Scene IV: Drop scene Cambaroora Road, moonlight after storm—for convenience of bank-rooms scene to follow. Note: If She-Oak Creek scene continues, moon shines through rift in storm cloud. The thunderstorm was managed capitally in this case in Dampier's last version of "Robbery Under Arms"—hut on plain scene)

RUTH: What a dreadful thunderstorm. Are you wet, Jack?

JACK: Rather damp. It was heavy while it lasted.

RUTH: Oh! look, Jack! The roof of the *Star* office has blown off! Whatever shall you do?

JACK: The best I can, darling. The rain is over. There can't be much damage done.

RUTH: But you sleep there. Where will you go tonight?

JACK: To one of the hotels. I'll be alright. Don't you worry.

RUTH: But I must. You've got a bad cold and you are wringing wet. Listen, Jack—Aunt's away for a holiday, and he won't be home till late. Come and dry yourself at the kitchen fire. I left the kettle on and I want you to have a good hot cup of coffee.

JACK: I can get that at the Nugget, dearie.

RUTH: But you can get whisky at the Nugget too.

JACK: I have promised, Ruth.

RUTH: Yes, Jack, I know, but poor Father used to drink, and I know what it is. I want you to get dry and have a good hot cup of coffee before you go to the Nugget. Do so for my sake, Jack.

JACK: But your uncle? We're not over-friendly.

RUTH: He'll be out till all hours. And—Jack—What does it matter? Do you love me?

JACK: What does it matter if *he* knows. Come, Ruth, I'll do as you wish.

(Exit)

Scene IV

Ruth's bedroom and dining room at the bank, as per plan [rough pencil sketch showing four rooms, two each side of a central corridor]

RUTH: You must take off your boots and dry them at the fire, Jack. Wait a minute *(goes to cupboard—or goes to her room with a candle—gets slippers and straightens up her hair and collar at glass, while Jack does same at glass over mantelpiece in dining room)* Here's a pair of slippers I worked for poor father. You put them on while your boots are drying. *(Love bus.)* Don't Jack, I must get you your coffee.

JACK: Plenty of time to hurry when I come home and growl when dinner's not ready.

RUTH: *(Bustling round table. N.B. If this does not fit in with the time, let the table be set for tea when the scene opens)*

Oh, you'll never do that, Jack! It will always be like this when we're married, won't it, dear? *(Hands him his coffee)*

JACK: I hope it will be a great deal better than this, darling.

RUTH: I'd be happy in a tent with you, dear. So long as you kept good. And I know you will, for my sake.

JACK: And so long as the tent didn't leak.

RUTH: I don't like you at all. Here, let me hang your overcoat by the fire to dry. *(Hangs coat on chairback)* What fell out of your pocket, dear? *(picks up brown paper parcel and puts it on the table)*

JACK: That question almost makes me feel as if we were married already, Ruth. I am my own machinist. I'm trying to tinker up my old printing press, and those are some tools I bought for it today.

RUTH: Another cup of coffee, Jack?

JACK: No thanks, darling.

RUTH: You can smoke if you like, dear—Uncle does.

JACK: You'll make a splendid little wife. But it's a bad start. I might want to smoke in bed afterwards.

RUTH: Well you can smoke tonight, can't you?

JACK: But after we're married I mean.

RUTH: If you talk such nonsense I'll have to send you home.

JACK: *(Draws her to him and kisses her)* I wish we were both at home now, darling. Don't you?

RUTH: I—I don't know. Don't ask stupid questions, I wish we were both away from here. *(Starts clearing table)*

JACK: We will be soon, if I can sell the *Star*.

(They plan life in a suburban cottage if there's time)

(Taking copy of Star *from pocket)* It will be like this, Ruth, after tea when we're married a year or so. *(Spreads paper in front of him and leans back comfortable. As he opens paper, letters, copy, bills, etc. fall out)*

RUTH: Oh! You couldn't be so cruel, Jack. *(Goes round to the back of his chair, and leans over him as he gathers up papers)*

(Aside) One's in a woman's handwriting too. I'd like to know what's in it.

(Aloud) What's in the *Star*, Jack? *(Points to article in the paper)*

JACK: Nothing to interest you, Ruth.

RUTH: But everything you write interests me, Jack—at least it does now.

JACK: *(Kissing her)* Some city swindlers, or spoilers, are trying to work up a bogus mining boom in Cambaroora. But I think I've exploded that.

RUTH: You good, clever boy! Let me read it.

Jack: No, I'm ashamed of it. I've been writing wretchedly lately.

RUTH: Nonsense, dear, let me read it. *(Takes paper. Reads)* We—we. Who's "we", Jack?

JACK: A newspaperman's term for one man's opinion. It was I. It's you and I now. It will mean *she*, no doubt, by-and-by.

RUTH: You nasty fellow. I don't like you. *(Reads)* "We have been shown the prospectus of an alleged Cambaroora gold mining company. Capital unlimited, etc. After the usual preliminaries common to such swindling advertisements, the Promoters have the unlimited cheek to assert that there is upwards of a thousand pounds' worth of machinery on the ground. Now, the only machinery at present on this field is an old-time windlass—and a very good one by the way—engineered by our honest old friend, Pinter, who is never happy unless he is putting down a shaft, and whom we wish every success." *(Breaking off)* Do you know a man named Sawkins, Jack?

JACK: Yes, I know him of old. He's at the bottom of this swindle no doubt. In another article, on professional spoilers that infest a country town, I gave him—in a way he cannot mistake—a pretty strong hint to clear out. He's the sort of man that old diggers of the Pinter school would have given an hour to clear off the field, perhaps less.

RUTH: But Uncle knows him.

JACK: I'm sorry to hear that.

RUTH: He brings him here very often lately. I hate that man!

JACK: I wonder at it. I hope your uncle's not mixed up in this business. But never you mind, dear. It won't matter to us. *(Love bus.)*

RUTH: *(Reads)* "Cambaroora has had a fairly clean record up to the present time." *(Clock strikes eleven. Both start up)*

JACK: That's the present time, dearie. I must go.
(Takes coat)

RUTH: Oh, Jack. I never thought it was so late.

JACK: Never mind, Ruth. Soon the clock will make no

Act I

difference to us. *(Love bus.)*

RUTH: We'll be so happy, dear. I know we will.

JACK: If it lies in a man's power, I will make you the happiest little woman in Australia.

RUTH: But are you happy, Jack?

JACK: Very happy, my darling. *(Takes her in his arms)*

BROWN: *(Outside)* You're alright, old man. Mind the fence. Stay where you are and I'll go round through the back door and let you in.

RUTH: Oh, Jack! There's Uncle, and someone with him, and he's been drinking! Whatever shall we do? *(Locks back door)*

JACK: Nothing; face him. I'll talk to him.

RUTH: But he's been drinking! I know what his temper is! I didn't like to tell you, Jack—but he doesn't like you. Quick, get into the passage, Jack. Don't let there be a row—for my sake.

JACK: Sawkins is with him. I'd best not meet him, for your sake, or his if it were worth anything.

RUTH: *(Pushing him into her room)* Go in there and wait. They'll be drunk or asleep in half an hour, and then I'll let you out quietly.

(Loud knock at back door. Ruth sees Jack's boots by the fire, snatches them up, hurries back to room and hands them in to Jack)

BROWN: Open the damned door! What the devil is this? Ruth! *(Ruth opens the door to Brown)* I thought you were in bed. What the devil did you lock the door for?

RUTH: You can't expect me to stay here alone with the door open, Uncle.

BROWN: Well, why the devil didn't you open it when I knocked?

(Goes through passage to front door)

JACK: *(Solus)* I can't stand this!

(Throws down coat and starts out, Ruth pushes him back, closes door and locks it. Brown brings Sawkins in)

SAWKINS: 'Ello Ruth. *(Ruth ignores him)*

BROWN: Are you deaf, Ruth—or blind? Don't you see Mr Sawkins?

RUTH: Yes, I see him

BROWN: Then, damn it! Be civil to him, he's my guest.

SAWKINS: That will do, Brown, let the girl alone, I don't mind.

BROWN: But *I* do. Look here, my lady! You've insulted Mr Sawkins twice today by passing him like dirt in the street when he raised his hat to you.

RUTH: Mr Sawkins insulted me twice in the street today, Uncle, by raising his hat to me.

BROWN: What! Who do you think you are? A pauper that I fed and clothed and brought up and this is the thanks I get. Shake hands with Mr Sawkins and beg his pardon, or out of this house you go tomorrow. Do you think I'll have my guests insulted by any of my wife's relations who happen to be loafing on me at the time?

RUTH: And I'll be insulted in no man's house. I've stood it too long. I won't stand it from you, Uncle, even though drink be the excuse, and do you think I'll put up with it from a cad like that, who leers at me in the public street and calls me by my Christian name?

(Jack is tugging at handle of Ruth's door)

SAWKINS: You'd stand it from a man like—like Mister—John—Drew, for instance, me dear.

(Ruth takes cup of tea, and flings it, tea and all, in his face)

BROWN: You she-devil! *(Is restrained by Sawkins)*

SAWKINS: Never mind, Brown. No harm done. These Australian bush girls are taken that way sometimes.

RUTH: I am an Australian bush girl, and I'm proud of it. *(Takes riding whip from side-board. Jack snatches door open)*

Speak to me again and you'll get something sharper than a cup of tea across your face!

BROWN: Go to your room.

RUTH: Yes, and tomorrow I'll go from your house.

(Goes out, meets Jack about to rush into dining room, pushes him back into her room. She stands by the door, sobbing, he comforts her. Brown sits down, rather sobered)

SAWKINS: Never mind, Brown, all in a lifetime. Have you got a drink in the house? *(Brown gets bottle and glasses from sideboard, and pours out drinks)* Here's success to our ventures. *(Brown takes small box with revolver in it from sideboard and puts it on table)* What have you got there, Brown?

BROWN: A revolver. *(Sawkins starts out of his chair)* That's alright, Sawkins. It's a new one I got by post today from Sydney. There are a lot of rough characters knocking around and my old pistol shoots too much like a boomerang to please me.

SAWKINS: Is that thing loaded?

BROWN: No.

SAWKINS: Then be careful with it. I was shot once before with a gun that wasn't loaded.

BROWN: Well, I'm going to load it now, and put it away, so you can rest easy. So long as you don't get shot by one of those little guns of your own that you load yourself, you're alright. *(Loads revolver and puts it away in a drawer)*

SAWKINS: *(Aside)* He's getting nasty now. The drunken fool's beginning to see that he told me too much of his private business this evening. Let him snarl, I've got the whip hand of him, and I'll pull him up with a round turn presently. *(Takes up* Star *and runs his eye over it. Suddenly reads with interest)*

SAWKINS: I hope you've found something to edify you in the *Star*.

BROWN: *(Sullenly handing paper to Brown)* Yes, and

something to edify you too.

BROWN: *(Reads)* What the devil's this? Curse that meddling fool Drew. How did he get hold of this? How did he get his information?

SAWKINS: Same as all journalists do—the same as the police do—from some ordinary fool. Curse him I say. Damn all journalists. He nearly ruined me once before—but I'll be even with him yet.

(Ruth and Jack attentive)

BROWN: Well, this finishes it, I suppose. That paragraph will go to the right quarter.

SAWKINS: Wrong quarter, you mean, for us. Couldn't you manage to get a libel action brought against him?

BROWN: No grounds. Besides, we're not fools.

SAWKINS: Buy up his debts and sell him off.

BROWN: Town's not civilized yet for that sort of thing. Besides, where's the money?

SAWKINS: Better drop it then, and start something else.

BROWN: But we can't drop it. I—we must have money at once. I told you so tonight. If I can't get the money I'm ruined. And mark me, Sawkins, you're in the same boat. You know what I mean? Go back to Sydney and do all you can before that paragraph gets round. I'll stay and look after Pinter and that painter fool. I'll fix him too.

SAWKINS: Alright. We'll talk about it in the morning. I'm full up of it tonight and dead tired.

BROWN: I'll sort out that girl and get her to make you a shake-down on the sofa.

SAWKINS: No thanks. Here's a rug—I'm alright. Go to bed, old man, and sleep over it. *(Brown locks side door, takes key out, takes revolver from drawer)*

BROWN: Good-night Sawkins. You'll find the whisky and soda on the sideboard.

SAWKINS: Thanks. Good-night.

Act I

(Brown turns down lamp and goes to his room)

JACK: He has locked the back door and left Sawkins in the room. I must get out by your window, Ruth. *(Tries window. The sash is jammed)*

RUTH: Yes, the wet weather makes it fast. You can't shift it. You must sneak out the front door—or wait till you're sure Sawkins is asleep. Uncle's rather deaf, you know. Oh, Jack! It's all my fault!

JACK: don't be frightened, dearie. I'll get out alright. *(Slips off slippers)* Good-night, Ruth. *(Kisses her. She pushes him gently into passage. He stands listening, overcoat on arm, boots in hand. Drops boot accidentally)* Damn the boot.

(Ruth draws him back into room. Sawkins rouses and listens.)

SAWKINS: *(Drowsily)* Brown's a long while thinking about turning in. I'd give five pounds for his thoughts. I don't like a partner of mine to think too hard when he ought to be in bed. Looks suspicious.

(Lies down again. Jack steps into passage, followed by Ruth, hears a noise, pushes Ruth back in to room, and is confronted by Brown who comes from his room, revolver in hand)

BROWN: What's this? Who are you? Sawkins? Speak! Stand where you are or I'll fire! Help! Burglary! Help! Sawkins!

(Ruth reels against the table, or chair, or bed, or open door, and clutches it for support. Jack stands a moment as if paralysed. Sawkins jumps up and gets poker, or life preserver, or ruler. Note: attention must be drawn to weapon earlier in evening)

JACK: *(Aside)* I must make a dash of it for Ruth's sake.

(Rushes at Brown, struggle during which revolver goes off. Ruth screams and falls. Jack makes through dining room to side door, while he is trying to open it he is struck down from behind by Sawkins. Brown comes in holding wrist)

SAWKINS: Are you hurt?

BROWN: No, just grazed. You'd better go for the police. I'll stand over him.

SAWKINS: See, who it is first. *(Turns Drew over)*

Both: Jack Drew!

SAWKINS: Brown, your cash is short.

BROWN: What the devil do you mean?

SAWKINS: Don't be a damned fool. Now's your chance or never. Quick, man, get your wits about you. How much is there in the safe in gold?

BROWN: About five hundred.

SAWKINS: Quick, man, jump! That shot will bring someone. Bring the gold from the safe. Leave the door open. Stop, look to the girl!

(Brown looks in Ruth's room)

BROWN: She's alright. She's fainted.

SAWKINS: Leave the safe door open. Bring me the keys and the gold. *(Brown hesitates)* Do it, you fool! Act now, or it might mean five years for you. It'll be £250 each for us and your books squared. Jump now and leave the rest to me.

(Brown goes to office)

SAWKINS: Brown doesn't know that the D's will be on my track in a week. That five hundred will give me a start and take me clear of the country. Brown must trust it to me, he's in my hands. And I'll be even with you, you cursed dog *(Kicks Drew with his foot)* And your lady friend too.

(Brown returns to room with keys and gold. Sawkins puts parcel of gold under sofa cushion—or as arranged on stage—and slips keys in Drew's pocket)

SAWKINS: He must have been in twice, remember and hid the gold. He took the keys from your room. Here they come. Use your wits now. Go and open the door. Stay! The revolver is his—you never saw it before, remember.

(Loud knocks at front door. Brown opens it. Enter

Mullaney, Cameron, Doctor Lebinski)

MULLANEY: What's this, Brown?

BROWN: Burglary! Come here! We've caught him!

MULLANEY: Why—it's Drew. Is he shot?

SAWKINS: No, only stunned. Look, he's coming round.

DOCTOR: Bring water. There's some blunder here, Mullaney.

BROWN: No room for a mistake, I'm sorry to say. He woke me with the noise he made and I caught him in the passage with his boots in his hand.

(Ruth, who has been recovering in her room, staggers to her feet and towards the door)

JACK: *(Resting on the Doctor's arm)* Where am I?

SAWKINS: That's what you've got to explain.

MULLANEY: Howld yet tongue, sir! I'll ask all the questions that's wanted.

JACK: What—what—oh, I remember.

DOCTOR: For God's sake, tell me what is the meaning of this, Jack. How came you here in this state? *(Jack is silent)*

MULLANEY: Speak, man. What have you got to say for yourself?

JACK: Nothing!

MULLANEY: Nothing?

(Brown slips away to the office. Constable Cameron takes packet from overcoat)

MULLANEY: What's this? Tools! Cold chisel, screw-wrench, screw-driver. Saints preserve us but this looks black for yer friend, Doctor.

DOCTOR: God! This is terrible. Speak, Jack—speak for God's sake.

MULLANEY: Best let him howld his tongue for the present, Doctor. Is yer safe arlright, Brown? Where's Brown?

BROWN: *(Rushing from office and feigning great excitement)* The safe's open and nine hundred in gold gone.

He must have been here twice tonight, or else he has an accomplice. My keys are gone too, from my room.

MULLANEY: You had no right to go into the office without me. I'm in possession now. Search him, Cameron.

CAMERON: *(Taking keys from Jack's pocket)* Here are the keys, sir.

MULLANEY: I kicked something in the passage, go and pick it up.

(Cameron brings revolver)

Is that yours, Brown?

(Sawkins nudges Brown energetically)

BROWN: No, I never saw it before.

JACK: It's a lie. This is a conspiracy.

MULLANEY: Then what were you doing here? *(Jack is silent)* I warn ye that what ye say will be used against ye in evidence.

RUTH: Oh, Uncle—that's the new revolver—

BROWN: What? Are you mixed up in this business?

MULLANEY: Be careful, Brown. You've been drinking.

RUTH: Oh! Jack—Jack.

(Doctor Lebinski catches her in his arms)

MULLANEY: Jack Drew! If ye can clear yerself shpeak up now!

SAWKINS: Perhaps the tools and keys got into his pocket by accident while he was spending a quiet evening with his lady love.

(Jack knocks Sawkins down and is secured by Mullaney and Cameron. Doctor Lebinski starts to carry Ruth off)

BROWN: Where are you taking that girl, Lebinski?

DOCTOR: Where she will be treated as she deserves and protected. Not treated like a dog.

BROWN: Then don't send her back here again. She and Drew and a pair in this matter, and—

JACK: It's a damned lie! This is the first time tonight that I

have seen Miss Wilson.
> BROWN: Then what were you doing here?
> JACK: Robbing the bank! You cowardly cur!
> MULLANEY: Silence!

CURTAIN

Act Two

Scene I

Corner of King and George Streets, Sydney. Evening. Newspapers, books, etc. on ledge of wall and pavement. (Pub corner) *Bloated, disreputable old woman to right, sitting on box against wall with baby, newspapers, trays of matches, bootlaces, etc. Mitchell as newsboy's agent, financial agent and general advisor to benighted swells, etc. etc. Bill Anderson, otherwise "The Nipper", a sharp newsboy.*

NIPPER: *(Dodging through crowd)* Noose! *Star*! 'Count of the double tragedy!

MITCHELL: *(Arranging papers)* Oh, well! I've drifted back into literature again, after all. Some people get on better at one thing and some people get on better at another. I seem to get on best when I'm doing nothing. As soon as I get into graft I get into debt—and the bigger the screw the deeper into debt I get. That's rum, ain't it? I think I was born to be a dude. I can keep square when I'm loafing and drifting round. There's nothing like travelling to keep out of debt. They say a rolling stone gathers no moss, but anyway, you can't gather any debts off of a rolling stone.

NIPPER: *Noose*! *Star*! 'Count of the sad occurrence!

MITCHELL: 'Count of the sad occurrence? 'Count of the double tragedy? Where's the 'count of millions of sad occurrences and tragedies that the newspapers never take any 'count of? First I get out of work in Cambaroora, and Jack Drew gets committed for trial and won't have me for a witness, and won't let any of his friends speak up for him and the trial gets postponed till next sessions. And poor Miss Wilson breaks her heart and gets brain fever, and goes out of her mind so she can't speak up for her sweetheart. And Mary takes service with the Doctor to help nurse Miss Wilson—and the doctor won't have his house painted , and that was a double tragedy. Poor old Pinter goes off his head and gets married to the cook at the Nugget—and when he comes to his senses again and escapes she sends the police after him for wife desertion. And I get a job, piece work, here in Sydney, and find myself with a month's work to do and nothing to draw for it. Some chaps get on the best in one place and some in another. I always seem to get on the best somewhere else. *(Counts his change)*

NIPPER: *Noose*! *Star*! 'Count of the ex-ee-cu-shun! 'Count of the double tragedy!

MITCHELL: Look here Nipper! There'll be a big single tragedy at this corner tonight if you don't look out. Come here, you young—

NIPPER: Well, what are you naggin' about now, Mitchell?

MITCHELL: You're short in your copper again, and what do you mean by giving me this?

(Holds out a bad sixpence)

NIPPER: What is it? A cronk tanner?

MITCHELL: Yes, you know what it is—and you're a cronk sprat. What do you mean by ringing it on me?

NIPPER: Well—'cos I wanted the change.

MITCHELL: You might have changed it in the pub.

NIPPER: Yes, an' the barman would have spotted it at wonst.

MITCHELL: So you thought it was safer to ring it on me. That's your idea of mateship is it, you blessed young scoundrel? I'll make a grease spot of you on the pavement if you try that on again! *(Swell steps towards old woman—who is digging with fingers in waistcoat pocket—to buy paper. Nipper runs in front of him holding out paper)*

NIPPER: Here y'are sir—*Noose*? *Star*? It's alright, mister, it's all the same, she's my mother.

SWELL: *(Giving him sixpence and taking paper)* Keep the change, my boy, and stick to your mother.

MITCHELL: The Nipper sticks to his mother anyway—so he must have some good points about him. I wonder if she *is* his mother, though. I can't spot the family likeness. Perhaps she's only an electioneering dodge of the Nipper's. Say, Nipper, is that really your old woman?

NIPPER: 'Corse she is. Straight iron. Least she says so, and she orter know. I was too young to remember. Anyways, she stuck to me when I was a kid, an' edercated me, an' bring me up—an' I'm not goin' ter sling her now.

MITCHELL: And how old are you now?

NIPPER: Dunno. My troubles! I'm old enough to suit meself an' that's all I want ter know. I'm jist in me prime.

MITCHELL: You must have been pretty smart when you was a young man, Nipper.

NIPPER: *(Reflectively—scratching his head)*

Yes, I was allers reckoned a smart kid. Say, Mitchell, see that bit of skirt acrost the street?

MITCHELL: Which one?

NIPPER: The piece lookin' this way, with the striped blouse an' the red fakement in her hat.

MITCHELL: Yes.

NIPPER: Well, I'm travellin' with her jist now. I wanter run acrost an' have a pitch with her for a minit. Just keep an eye on my ole woman, will yer, while I'm gone, an' see that she don't go for a beer? *(To his mother)* Here, shake yerself up, ole gal, an' look after yer papers. I'll be back in a minit.

(Exit—or crosses the street and converses with a young larrikiness)

MITCHELL: Oh, here's a go. Mary—of all the girls in the world. Just my luck. If she think I'm a news-merchant she'll cut me dead.

Act II

(Puts on overcoat, fixes collar, takes a walking stick from behind papers)

(To old woman) Keep your eye on my stand for a minute, Mrs Anderson.

(Old woman nods, Mitchell rests carelessly on his stick behind him as a gentleman of leisure.)

(Enter Mary)

MARY: Why, it's Jack!

MITCHELL: Why, Mary! *(They shake hands)*

MARY: Why, whatever are you doing down here, Jack? I thought you'd gone up country.

MITCHELL: Oh, I just came down to have a fly round. Whatever are you doing here, Mary?

MARY: Oh, I came down with Doctor Lebinski and his sister and Ruth—Miss Wilson. She's been ill ever since that bank affair, you know. Brain fever—she's been out of her mind, poor thing. The Doctor brought her down to see if the change would do her any good; but it won't.

MITCHELL: Why not?

MARY: Because she's breaking her heart for someone.

MITCHELL: Oh I see.

MARY: You know he escaped.

MITCHELL: What?

MARY: Yes.

MITCHELL: Look at that now. Never heard of it—and I'm one of the fountainheads of the great Australian press. They must have kept it pretty quiet.

MARY: Why, are you on a paper, Jack?

MITCHELL: *(Aside)* Confound it, I put my foot in it.

(To Mary) Yes.

MARY: What paper?

MITCHELL: I'm in the General Press Agency. But ever mind that now. Tell me all about it, Mary. *(Aside)* Here's the Nipper, confound him. This is just the sort of situation he'll spread himself out to improve.

MARY: It happened three weeks ago. You knew Jack Drew was committed for trial at Binalong, and had to be taken there in the coach?

MITCHELL: Yes.

MARY: Constable Mullaney took him. I don't think Mullaney believes that Jack Drew did rob the bank.

MITCHELL: Nor I, either.

MARY: Nor anyone in Cambaroora. They think that Brown and Sawkins' yarn is a very fishy one. That Jack Drew was drunk and blundered into the bank, or something of that sort. But he wouldn't speak, and Ruth was too ill. I've got my own ideas about it.

MITCHELL: Well, what about the escape?

MARY: Mullaney was taking him to Binalong in the coach. They say Mullaney wouldn't handcuff him. The coach stopped at the Halfway House.

MITCHELL: Just so. Go ahead, Mary.

MARY: And when they went to start again, one of the wheels came off. There was a pin, or cap missing.

MITCHELL: Was there?

MARY: Yes, Pinter's son Jim was at the Halfway House.

MITCHELL: Oh! That explains it. Perhaps he greased the axle.

MARY: So he did. He was working in the stables and he heard one of the wheels squeak and greased it.

MITCHELL: That explains it.

MARY: Pinter's son Jim's horse was tied up in front of the hotel.

MITCHELL: Just so.

MARY: And in the confusion when the coach broke down, Jack Drew took his chance and jumped on Pinter's son Jim's horse and was away like the wind. And Pinter's son Jim swore after Drew terrible, they say, about losing his horse. And

Pinter's son Jim jumped on the only other saddled horse that was there and galloped away like mad after Jack.

MITCHELL: Just so. Jim always hated to lose a horse if it didn't belong to someone else. Is Pinter's son Jim back yet?

MARY: That's the strangest part of it. He's never been heard of since. But they say that his sweetheart Kate—the barmaid at the Nugget—has a pretty good idea where he is.

MITCHELL: Very likely. Perhaps he's following Jack Drew across the Never-Never Country.

MARY: And Brown—the bank manager—lost his billet.

MITCHELL: How was that?

MARY: It came out he was away drinking that night.

MITCHELL: Serve him right. Where are you living, Mary?

MARY: I mustn't tell you.

MITCHELL: Why? Are the police after him too? I'm beginning to think I got into bad company up the country.

MARY: It isn't that. I've got an idea that he thinks somebody might come to look for somebody and get caught—you know—

MITCHELL: That's just the way of it. The first thing a man thinks of when he escapes from gaol is finding the woman. That's how half of them get caught.

MARY: Hush! We musn't talk in the street.

MITCHELL: We musn't kiss, either, that's the worst of it.

MARY: Go along with you, who wants to kiss?

MITCHELL: Look here, Mary. I'll ask you a straight question to prevent mistakes. Are you in love with me?

MARY: And I'll give you a straight answer, to prevent mistakes—no I'm not, I'm in love with someone else.

MITCHELL: Who?

MARY: Pinter's son Jim.

MITCHELL: That's the way of it. Oh, why wasn't I born a scamp! I'll go bushranging. I'll loaf around and drink and fight and gamble, like Pinter's son Jim, and there'll be a horse missing whenever I go away; and then some girl will fall in love with me.

MARY: You'd better take off your coat and put away that stick, and look after your papers, Jack. *(Mitchell collapses)* And if you're down about Lady Macquarie's Chair about five o'clock tomorrow evening you might get a bite, Jack. *(Mitchell revives)*

(Exit Mary)

MITCHELL: That's the way of 'em. Knock you down one minute and fill you full of joy the next. *(Kicks Nipper, who is deep in a Deadwood Dick story. Nipper takes it as a matter of course and picks up his bundle of papers)*

NIPPER: *Noose! Star!* 'Count of the sad occurrence in Woolloomooloo!

(Enter Sawkins and Brown—passing by)

SAWKINS: Well, where shall we go? We can't talk here. Shall we go to a pub?

BROWN: No, we might talk too much there. Come into the park to Lady Macquarie's Chair.

MITCHELL: Well, what next? Here, Nipper!

NIPPER: Well, what's the trouble now?

MITCHELL: See them two toffs?

NIPPER: The one with the tall hat and the go-to-blazes coat, and the one with the square-cut and boxer?

MITCHELL: Yes, fox 'em and put me up to their game.

NIPPER: How much is it worth?

MITCHELL: A bob.

NIPPER: Rats! Say half-a-caser.

MITCHELL: Alright, go along.

NIPPER: Keep an eye on my old woman. *Noose! Star!*

(Exit Nipper after Sawkins and Brown)

MITCHELL: And here's my boss, Mr Putty. I'm having an "at home" tonight.

(Enter Mr Putty)

PUTTY: Look here, Mitchell, what do you mean by leaving that job before you finished it?

MITCHELL: Well, I couldn't finish it before I left it.

PUTTY: You drew two pounds last Saturday and there's a fortnight's work to do.

MITCHELL: And only thirty shillings to draw on it.

PUTTY: If I'd have known you weren't going to finish the job, I wouldn't have paid you that two pounds.

MITCHELL: Then it would have been all the worse for me. That's exactly why I didn't like to tell you.

PUTTY: Well I can't help it, if I hadn't to take jobs so cheap I wouldn't be in the position I'm in today.

MITCHELL: And if I hadn't to do work so cheap I wouldn't be in the position I am tonight. But me and that position ain't going to go along together any longer.

PUTTY: Well, Mitchell, we won't quarrel. You're not doing anything in the daytime, and I don't want to take on a new hand. Finish the job and I'll make it a couple of quid more and lend you a hand this week.

MITCHELL: It's a bargain!

PUTTY: Right you are. Come and have a drink.

MITCHELL: Keep your eye on my papers, Mrs Anderson.

(Exit Mitchell and Putty—into pub)

Side Show

Enter Brown and Jones—two boozers.

BROWN: Yesh, ole man—but the question is *hic!* warril yer wife shay *hic!* Imeansh, what'll yer shay to—the—yer wife?

JONES: Thash all ri'. She'll *hic!* do all the shaying. Shay—ole man. What'll *your* wife shay?

BROWN: Norra—word. She knows berra. I'm *hic!* master in me own house.

JONES: Sho-my. I'll see who's boss. I'll be *hic!* mas'r-in-m-own housh. I mean to *hic!* perform when I *hic!* g'home t'night. Thish sorter nonsense gone on long enough with my wife. I'll *hic!* shtand on my dig—dig—dig—dignity! *(Slips down on pavement)*

BROWN: *(Helping him up)* Stand on yer *hic!* feet, ole man, first. *(Hiccough all through)*

JONES: I'll stand on my *hic!* dignity! *(Starts taking off coat. Brown puts it on again)*

JONES: *(Furiously)* I'll be insulted by no man. *(Suddenly changing)* Eshept my ole chums. *(Shaking Brown's hand)* Never mind. Come and have a drink with me, ole man.

BROWN: Pointing to penny-in-the-slot weighing machine) Look at the *hic!* time—twelvsh o'clock.

JONES: You're seeing double. It's only shix er sheven. You're *hic!* screwed, ole man—come 'n' have a whisky an' shoda.

BROWN: Right y'are ole man. Man must have a little rec—rec—rec—crashion. A woman can't understand these thingsh. Have-a-night once in a while. Come along, ole man, we'll make a night of it, come on. I know where thersh a bar with some orright girls, come on.

JONES: Right y'are. We'll make a night of it and damn the *hic!* world. Right turn! Quick marsh!

MRS BROWN: *(Meeting them)* James!

BROWN: What—eh?—who—? Beg pardinsh, m'dear! 's alright, Maria— 's alright, m'dear. I was jusht comin' home, Maria. Just met Jones—Mr Jones, Maria.

MRS BROWN: You ought to be jolly well ashamed of yourself, Mr Jones. How dare you take my husband out and—

JONES: Good night, Brown. I'm off.

(Runs into arms of second hard-faced woman, Mrs Jones, who enters right)

MRS JONES: John!

JONES: Eh!—Oh, it's you, Sarah. I—I—I'm just comin' home m'dear.

MRS JONES: I know you are, come along!

JONES: I just met Brown m'dear.

MRS JONES: I know you did.

JONES: There he ish with Mrs Brown. Berra speak to Mrs Brown, Sarah—m' *hic!* m'dear.

MRS JONES: *(Loud)* He ought to be ashamed of himself.

MRS BROWN: He's no worse than your husband, Mrs Jones.

MRS JONES: It's him that takes my husband drinking.

MRS BROWN: What do you mean by that, ma'am?

(While they wrangle, Brown and Jones make signs to each other behind the women's backs, and slip down side door into a wine cellar)

MRS BROWN: *(Breaking down)* As if I haven't got enough to bear without this. I never expected this from you, Mrs Jones.

MRS JONES: Well, one's as bad as the other. Don't mind what I said, Mrs Brown.

MRS BROWN: I'll give it to my James when I get him home.

MRS JONES: And I'll give it to my John such a talking to as he won't forget for many a long day. *(Turns left)* Why, the wretch! Where is he?

MRS BROWN: *(Turns right)* The wretch! Where is he?

MRS JONES: I know where they've gone. You run around that way and meet me in Castlereagh Street. Just wait till I catch John. I'll make him remember it the longest day he lives.

(Exit right and left. Re-enter Brown and Jones from wine cellar in convulsions of laughter)

BROWN: Ha! Ha! Ha! Never laughed sho mush in me life. I worked orright, didn't I?

JONES: So'd I. I only shed what I shed t'her t'put her off the shent.

BROWN: Same here.

BOTH: It worked grand. Come along, ole man! We won't go home till morning!

(They dance. Enter policeman)

POLICEMAN: Come along, both of you. *(Takes them)*

BROWN: Fryin' pan inter the firesh!

JONES: Damn if I know sho mush about that. Never shay die, ole man.

(Exit Constable and Brown and Jones)
(Enter Mitchell from hotel and Nipper from street)

MITCHELL: Well?

NIPPER: One cove named Sawkins. T'other bloke named Brown. Cronk I think. Might be peelers, but I dunno 'em. Pitch about a feller that smoked from quod up the kentry—named Drew. They wanter git on his track. Reckon he'll make after a gal named Druth that came down here larst week with a doctor named Blue-Wincey—or some such blarsted name. Wanter find out where Druth and Blue-whisky is stoppin'. Sawkins is goin' to try tomorrow. Where's the half-caser?

MITCHELL: Here it is. Did you find out where they're stopping?

NIPPER: City—Coffee Palace.

MITCHELL: Help me to clear up, I'm off tonight.

(Nipper, Mitchell and old woman clear up)

MITCHELL: Well, Nipper, how's the gender?

NIPPER: She chucked me.

MITCHELL: How's that?

NIPPER: How'm I ter know? Yer can't git at what a petticoat's up to.

MITCHELL: That's true.

NIPPER: I'm goin' up the kentry nixt week.

MITCHELL: How's that?

NIPPER: I've got a sort of uncle shearin' in a shed t'other side of Bourke. He'll see me through. I'm goin' up to make a cheque.

MITCHELL: Bully for you, Nipper. I'll see you before you go.

NIPPER: That's alright.

MITCHELL: *(Aside)* I wish Mary had told me where she lived. But I'll see her tomorrow and look after Messrs Sawkins and Brown tonight. I reckon I've got a bite this time.

(Exit all with papers etc.)

(Author's Note: *I had an idea of putting in the Jones's Alley Shifting Scene. But think there won't be room)*

Scene II

Doctor Lebinski's lodgings. Doctor on lounge, ill. Ruth in chair by his side.

RUTH: Do you feel better now, Doctor?

DOCTOR: Yes, Ruth, I am much easier. But you are fretting again, girl! You must not do that. It will do no good. I still believe in the simple old saying: "All things will come right in the end".

RUTH: I'm trying not to fret, but it's hard.

DOCTOR: Then open your heart to me, my girl, it may do you good.

RUTH: I'm thinking of Jack, Doctor.

DOCTOR: I know you are, poor girl.

RUTH: Hunted about the bush—an outlaw—and all for my sake.

DOCTOR: His own fault! But he will be all right, Ruth. Pinter's son Jim is a thorough bushman, and he will stick to him. It is best for Jack's sake that he is out of the way—best for him and best for you. I promised you, Ruth—to soothe you when you were ill—that you should go to the court and give evidence for him. His escape was the best thing that could have happened at the time.

RUTH: But, Doctor, you must not think me ungrateful, but why do you always seem to speak coldly of Jack? His is the noblest heart that ever beat, and he is suffering for my sake now. Why will you not let me go to the police and clear him? Oh, Doctor, you surely do not believe that he had anything to do with that money?

DOCTOR: No, I told you that I put a detective on Sawkins' track. When the mystery of the gold is cleared up Jack may come forward and explain his presence in the bank as best he can. He can say he was drunk and did not know where he was—as he should have done in the first place. But, Ruth, I am determined to one thing—and you have sworn to me, by the memory of your dead mother, to obey and be guided by me in this matter—I am determined that you shall not help him to clear himself at the expense of your good name. No man that ever lived is worth that.

RUTH: My good name? Oh, Doctor, what do you mean? What harm have we done? What is there to hide or be ashamed of? Jack would not speak because he thought people might think there was something in that man's—and I cannot call him my uncle—in that man's drunken, brutal suggestion that I had something to do with the robbery. Or—oh, Doctor, I see it all now! Jack thought that the vile, lying, mischief-making tongues in that country hole might make harm out of the fact that he was hiding in my room that night—that they would not believe the true story, that he was there for my sake to avoid a scene. Oh, what a vile, vicious world this is. I will delay no longer. I will go tomorrow to the police authorities and tell the truth.

(The Doctor starts up and claps his hand to his forehead)
Doctor! Oh, Doctor! Did you believe that that—

DOCTOR: No, Ruth, No! I—

RUTH: You are ill again, and it is my fault! Oh what a selfish, ungrateful girl I am. Come, you must lie down.

DOCTOR: No, it was only a spasm. I am all right now, Ruth, but we must not talk any more tonight. You are not strong, and I forbid it for your sake as well as mine. Come, Ruth, you must go to bed now and try to sleep.

RUTH: But I cannot leave you like this.

DOCTOR: You will do no good sitting up with me, only make yourself ill, and that will not help me. I must be quiet for a while. Go to your room. Mary will be in presently and I will send her to you. *(Leads Ruth to the door)* Good-night, my girl. Jack will be righted. I will decide in the morning what is

best to be done. Try to sleep now, for his sake. You will need your health and strength. Do not fret. I believe now, and to my bitter sorrow perhaps, in the homely old philosophy and simple faith that says, "forever the Right comes uppermost and ever is Justice done."
(Exit Ruth)

DOCTOR: Is it possible that I am mistaken—I a Doctor and a man of the world! Bah! What a false, paltry thing worldly wisdom is! Can it be possible that Ruth is deceiving me? Could she speak and look like that if the case is as I thought? But a woman will do anything to shield the man she loves—her whole nature will change. I wish I had five minutes with Jack Drew—I would know the truth, then, and know how to act.

(Enter Mary, hurriedly)

MARY: Oh, Doctor! I've been followed by a man!

DOCTOR: What?

MARY: A man, all muffled up and there was another man behind him.

DOCTOR: Perhaps it was Jack Mitchell. He is in Sydney.

MARY: *(Indignantly)* No! It was not Jack Mitchell.

DOCTOR: Well, Mary, I didn't mean—*(Bell rings)* Go down and see who it is.

(Exit Mary)

It is he. I knew he would find us out and come to us if he kept out of the hands of the police long enough. *What* am I to do? It is best for her to see him. She would go melancholy mad if she did not.

(Enter Mary)

MARY: Oh, Doctor, it's him! He—he wants to see you alone—I did get such a start.

DOCTOR: Then get over it now, as quick as you can. Bring him up quietly, and you go to Miss Wilson—shut all the doors. Not a word of this to her until I call you.

(Exit Mary)

Act II

My God! What am I to do now? Would it be better for her sake to have them married quietly, and tell as little of the truth as possible in court? Or let him, if he is a man, serve his sentence like a man. But no! If he were hound enough to wrong a girl like Ruth—if he were contemptible enough to take advantage of her under such circumstances—he would stick at nothing to clear himself, and he would make the girl's life a hell afterwards!

(Enter Jack Drew, stubby beard, rough clothes, cheap overcoat)

Jack Drew! Are you mad!

JACK: I heard that Ruth was ill—dying—is that true?

DOCTOR: You might be doing the right thing to kill her. How did you come here?

JACK: I did not intend to seek either you or Ruth. I came to Sydney to take my chances of getting out of the country. I came across country and have been riding—by night mostly—on Pinter's son Jim's horse. He came with me to the ranges and then made off Out Back. I saw Mary by accident, talking to Mitchell tonight, and overheard part of the conversation. I could bear my suspense and loneliness no longer—I felt that I must see you or Ruth for the last time—before I died to the world, so I followed Mary home.

DOCTOR: Jack Drew. I gathered part of the truth from Ruth's lips in her delirium. How much remains I do not know. This I know, that you are not a thief. Someone took the money from the safe—Sawkins or Brown might know something about that, but you do not. Whether you are a worse and more contemptible scoundrel your own heart will tell you.

JACK: What do you mean? Are you mad?

DOCTOR: No, I am not mad. Look here, Jack Drew. If you have wronged that girl, and if you have one spark of manhood left, plead guilty to the honester—the manlier crime—that you did not commit, and serve your sentence like the man you have not been yet. And know that your punishment, in any case, will be far more merciful than you deserve.

JACK: Wronged the girl! I understand you now! And this is the world of faith in friendship! This is the fruit of your worldly wisdom! I wronged Ruth by asking her to marry a vagabond like me. I wronged her, in my carelessness, thoughtlessness and selfishness by allowing her to put herself in a false position in the bank that night. But you—you of all the men in the world—believed me capable and guilty of taking that, that paltry advantage of Ruth's love and innocence—a thing that any country-town loafer and blackguard might do—and boast about afterwards. If I were a villain I would not be one of that contemptuous type.

DOCTOR: *(Holding out his hand)* Jack, Jack forgive me. I have wronged you both.

JACK: *(Taking Doctor's hand)* With all my heart, old man. The world is to blame, not you. But you have acted nobly for Ruth's sake.

DOCTOR: But why didn't you speak, my boy? It would have saved all this. And I left you to your fate! Thinking that you deserved it.

JACK: You could not have helped me, Doc. I could not have helped myself without handing Ruth over to the mercy of all the hags and blackguards in Cambaroora.

DOCTOR: But it might have been explained, and the police put on the track of the real criminal.

JACK: Explained! You should know the world better than that. No doubt all good Christians who heard of it would have taken a charitable view of the fact that Jack Drew, the careless, drinking vagabond of Cambaroora was in a respectable girl's bedroom after midnight. Damn the world, I say!

DOCTOR: I know it, Jack.

JACK: I did intend to pretend that I was drunk and blundered into the bank, but as things turned out I could not.

Act II

I had made up my mind to plead guilty at the trial, but when Pinter's son Jim offered me a chance at the Halfway House, I took it. And perhaps it was best—a month in gaol would have driven me mad. Now, Doc, it is for you to say whether it would be better for me to see Ruth or no. Use your professional judgement.

DOCTOR: Professional judgement does not cover these things. She is weak and ill, and the result of a shock, or of any excitement now, might prove fatal.

JACK: She has suffered enough for me. Tell her, Doc, that I am safe out of the country. And by-and-by, when she is stronger, tell her that I am dead, and at rest. Better that than that I should be a living shadow over her whole life. She is young, she will forget in time and be happy. Good-bye, Doc. *(Holds out his hand)*

DOCTOR: But, Jack! Where are you going? What shall you do? I cannot let you go like this—I must help you to hide and get away. *(Jack moves towards door. Doctor draws him back)* I will not let you go! Listen, Jack, Ruth will never forget, she will break her heart, I have a detective on Sawkins' track, and that bank affair might be cleared up any day. Perhaps it would be better for Ruth's happiness that you and she should be married quietly. I can have it done, and then we can face this thing out.

JACK: No, no, to ask her to marry an outlaw—a hunted man—

DOCTOR: *(Sinking into chair)* Listen, Jack, I am suffering from an old complaint that might kill me at any moment. Then what would become of Ruth? Better do as I say—Oh, God! By the love I bore her mother, show me, tell me what to do for my girl and my friend!

(Enter Ruth in dressing gown)
RUTH: Jack!
JACK: Ruth! My Darling!

(The Doctor falls back on lounge)
DOCTOR: Jack!
(Ruth and Jack go to his side)
JACK: Doc, what is it?
RUTH: Oh, Doctor!
DOCTOR: *(Gasping)* Only a passing pain…I'm better now. Don't be frightened, Ruth. You must leave us alone for a few minutes. I must speak to Jack. Go to your room, dear. I will send for you in five minutes.
(Jack leads Ruth to the door. Exit Ruth)
DOCTOR: Give me a glass of spirits from the cupboard yonder.
JACK: *(Getting spirits)* You must have a doctor. This will not do.
DOCTOR: No, all the doctors in the world could not help me now. It is the old trouble, heart disease. My time is close now, I feel it. Listen, as you love Ruth, and do not speak. If I pass out tonight you must get away before the doctor's and the undertaker's people come—or hide until after the funeral. I have a lawyer on your case and a detective man I can trust. One was a comrade of mine in Poland. If the detective succeeds he will get a hundred pounds. I have very little money left—but there should be a hundred over after the funeral expenses are paid. That must be kept in hand. Now, listen, Jack. There is money coming to me from Poland—a large sum. It goes to Ruth without conditions. It may be six months coming—not later. The necessary papers are with the lawyer and the German Consul. The lawyer's name and full information are with a letter to Ruth in my desk which she is to read…

Act II

[One page of the manuscript is missing at this point]

Scene III

Back Street. Enter Sawkins and Brown.

BROWN: How did you manage to find out where they lived so quickly?

SAWKINS: By a bare chance. After I left you I caught sight of that girl, Mary, going through Hyde Park, and followed her on the other side of the street. There was another man a few yards behind her all the way. I didn't take any particular notice of him until I saw him stop in front of the house where she went in, knock at the door, and go in after her. I'll take my oath it *was* Jack Drew.

BROWN: And what did you do then?

SAWKINS: There was a furnished room to let in the next house; I wanted an office and I wanted to watch things—so I saw the landlady and took that room.

BROWN: The devil you did! You won't catch me there! What did you do after that?

SAWKINS: I sent an anonymous note to the police station saying that there was a wanted man in that house.

BROWN: What good will that do?

SAWKINS: Can't you see? If Jack Drew and the Doctor get their heads together they might put the D's on our track in no time.

BROWN: But the harm's done now. The police mightn't notice the letter. They mightn't move in the matter till some time today. They take things easy sometimes.

SAWKINS: They get there just the same. I'll chance it anyway. There's five or six pounds a week coming in from that missing word competition of ours, and one or two other things I've got on. I'm not going to run away from that. You can if you like. You're not a particular friend of Drew's are you?

SAWKINS: Damn him! I'll see him hanged yet! He cost me

my billet!

SAWKINS: Well, look here, in case my note misfired last night, how would it be for you to go round to the police station and—

BROWN: What! I'll be damned if I'll do—

SAWKINS: What are you afraid of? You're the principal party interested. You lost your billet through the robbery. You're justified in moving in the matter.

BROWN: I tell you I won't be mixed up in it. Best leave it alone. You'll make a mess of it yet and get your fingers burnt if you're not careful.

SAWKINS: Leave me alone. I'll run quick enough when I scent danger. So-long—remember our appointment for this evening.

BROWN: Alright; you should have been a detective, Sawkins.

SAWKINS: I have been.

(Exit separately)
(Enter Mitchell)

MITCHELL: Well, I've got Putty's apron and brushes, and I've got an idea that that's all I'll see of him today. It's no use hunting for Doctor Lebinski's on my own, I'll have to wait till I see Mary tonight.

Scene IV

Room in Doctor Lebinski's lodgings. Jack Drew sitting at breakfast table, Ruth pouring out tea, etc.

RUTH: You must try to eat, Jack. You don't know what might be before you.

JACK: And you must sit down and have your breakfast too. You are trembling, and pale as death. Oh! what a mad selfish brute I was to come here last night, and bring this cloud of trouble on you and on my best friend!

RUTH: Don't, Jack. Oh it's cruel of you to talk like that. I was breaking my heart for you; and if I'd have known that you had been so near and gone away without seeing me I would never, never have forgiven you. It would have broken my heart, Jack.

JACK: My own true girl! And do you love me so much as that?

RUTH: You don't know how much a woman can love, Jack. Men can't realise it

(They stay apart as Mary enters with breakfast tray)

RUTH: How is the Doctor, Mary?

MARY: He's still asleep, miss. I took in his cocoa but thought it best to let him sleep.

RUTH: You did right.

(Exit Mary)

JACK: I think his plan is the best. I'll wait here till tonight, then take my chance to get Out Back the way I came. And, Ruth, whatever happens, you must abandon that foolish idea of going to the police and clearing me. It would be useless—it would do more harm than good at present. A good detective is at work on my behalf, and when the bank robbery is cleared up we will see what we can do. Promise me you'll do nothing foolish.

Act II

RUTH: I can't, Jack! If you are taken I'll speak.

JACK: You must promise me—I will not be taken.

(Enter Mary)

MARY: Oh, what will I do! You must hide! You must get away! There are two policemen in front watching the house. I saw them through the sitting room window!

(Ruth and Jack start up)

RUTH: Go to the Doctor's room, Jack, and hide in the wardrobe. Run!

JACK: No! I couldn't do that. It would be sacrilege. I've done enough harm as it is. I'll go out and give myself up.

RUTH: Then I'll go with you.

JACK: You will not. I tell you, you must not. If you love me you must obey me in this.

RUTH: I do love you, but I will not obey you in this. *(Bell rings)* They'll search the house. You can't hide here. Oh my God, help me think now! Jack, you must get out of the window and hide on the roof close to the wall till they're gone. This house is not overlooked. Get behind the chimneys. Quick, Jack! *(Pulls him toward window)*

MARY: Oh, there's someone on the roof outside.

RUTH: Oh! God help us—help me to save him!

JACK: God forgive me for bringing this trouble on those that love me!

(Mitchell appears at window with pot and brush)

MARY: Oh, it's Jack! Help us, Jack, the police are downstairs!

(Mitchell jumps into room, with bag containing painter's kit. Takes apron out of bag)

MITCHELL: Here, Jack! Put this on! *(Helps him with apron)* It's lucky Putty didn't turn up after all. Get out of the window! Take that pot and brush and go up those steps. Dust off that spouting and paint as if your life depended on it.

(Mitchell gets out after Jack and starts painting round

window outside)

RUTH: They're coming up!

(Exit Mary. Knock at door. Ruth admits two constables)
What does this mean, constable? What do you want here?

1ST CONSTABLE: Does Doctor Lebinski live here?

RUTH: My guardian died last night.

1ST CONSTABLE: Very sorry, miss, but we have orders to search these rooms for a suspected person.

RUTH: You've made a mistake.

1ST CONSTABLE: That may be, but we must do our duty. *(To Mitchell)* who are you?

2ND CONSTABLE: He's alright, sir. He's a painter working here, Oi know him.

MITCHELL: *(Aside)* I'm known to the police then. *(To Ruth)* Excuse me, miss, I didn't know you had trouble here or I wouldn't have started work. I'll take my man away to another job.

RUTH: Thank you.

1ST CONSTABLE: See who's outside, Murphy.

(2nd Constable looks out window and upwards, draws back clapping his hand to his eye)

1ST CONSTABLE: What's the matter with you?

2ND CONSTABLE: Oi've got a quart o' paint in me oi.

MITCHELL: My mate is a bit of a splasher. *(To Jack)* Look out, Bill, you're throwing paint in the eyes of the law.

(2nd Constable looks out, resting hand on sill and draws back disgusted, with paint on hands)

1ST CONSTABLE: It's only a painter.

MITCHELL: Only a painter? It's always "only a painter". I tell you there's no work that couldn't be finished without a painter.

1ST CONSTABLE: What about brasswork?

MITCHELL: Oh, well, brasswork wears a blue uniform sometimes and only needs white-washing occasionally.

Act II

1ST CONSTABLE: Come, Murphy, we're wasting time.

MARY: Well, you might be civil out of respect for the dead.

1ST CONSTABLE: We'll respect the dead if we find any, our work is with the living.

RUTH: Go with these men, Mary.

(Exit Mary and constables)

MITCHELL: Cheer up, Miss Wilson, I'll get him off alright. I must get him away from that window. *(Loud)* Come on, Bill, bring your pot and brushes and give me a hand with the ladder.

(Jack, in passing window, hurriedly kisses Ruth. Exit Jack and Mitchell. Re-enter [Mary and] constables, caps in hand)

1ST CONSTABLE: Very sorry indeed, miss, but we had to do our duty. There must be a mistake. I suppose there has been a doctor in attendance.

RUTH: Yes, Dr —— in this street.

1ST CONSTABLE: That's all right then. Good morning, miss.

(Exit constables)

MARY: *(At window)* They're safe. There they go with a ladder between them. My Jack will get him off and bring us word tonight.

RUTH: Oh Mary! I have no one now! *(Sinks down)*

MARY: *(Comforting her)* Oh, don't say that. There's God and me and my Jack, and Pinter's son Jim to help you.

CURTAIN

Act Three

Scene I

Machine shearing shed in full swing. "Wool Away!" "Tar!" "Sheep-Ho", etc. Jack Drew—known as "Macquarie"—and Pinter's son Jim—known as "Jim Moonlight"—are pen-mates in front. (Or open end of shed on one side so that the scene shows shed, hut, yards, etc.)

Big horned ram, in poor condition, just shorn.

Note: Author can arrange staging of "pens" and "shoots" and instruct in shearing, picking-up or any shed points.

SHEARER: Luk at 'im. Ain't he a beauty?
(Shoves ram down shoot. Enter Kate Kennedy disguised as a boy)
KATE: *(To Boss-over-the-board)* Any chance of a job?
BOSS: What are you? Shearer or rouseabout?
KATE: Greenhand.
BOSS: Alright, you can start picking. Here, Nipper, show this man how to pick up.
NIPPER: *(To Kate)* Come on you chap. Them's the men yer to pick up for. That one and that one and that one and that one, and that beggar there with the cross-eyed legs and red hair. Better put red raddle on the backs of their pants so's yer'll know 'em. Now this is the way yer pick up. Take the fleece like this, bring it over like this, over again, now put it here, wait till yer get two, then bring 'em to the table and I'll show you how to throw out. Get along now an' if yer not spry yer can take a walk and take yer swag along with yer. *(Knees, kicks or shoves Kate behind)*
KATE: *(Taking Nipper by hair)* Yer takes holt like that

(taking him by seat of pants) and like that *(hauling him over towards wool basket)* and yer fetches it over like that, over again *(throwing him head first into wool basket)* and yer throws it out like that.

(Shearers laugh. "Good for the jackaroo" "The Nipper's shorn at last", etc.)

(Smoke Ho!)

(Jim sitting sharpening shears. Kate comes behind Jim, stops and touches him on shoulder)

KATE: Jim.

JIM: *(Looks up and starts erect)* Why, Kate!

KATE: Hush!

(The Nipper has been taking stock of Kate and winks at audience. Jim seizes him by collar)

NIPPER: It's alright, Jim, I'm fly. I know a woman's hand in my hair when I feels it.

JIM: Can you get up some excitement outside, Nipper?

NIPPER: How much?

JIM: A bob.

NIPPER: Alright.

(Exit)

JIM: What is it, Kate?

KATE: Constable Cameron. He was transferred to the border last week, He might be out here any day. There's a warrant out for you, Jim, I came to give you the office.

JIM: A warrant? What for?

KATE: That horse at the Halfway House.

JIM: Oh, is that all! Why I let that horse go the same night.

KATE: Well, he never came back.

JIM: The fools! I suppose the horse went down the river to Cattle Creek, where he was bred. It's all right, Kate. They can only get an illegally-using charge against me, anyway.

KATE: It's all wrong, Jim. They'll have you in for horse-stealing. Clear out at once.

(Cry of "Fight!" "The Nipper and young Sandy!" "Ten to one on the Nipper" The men rush out)

JIM: I'll see to that. How did you get here, Kate?

KATE: I rode across country. I started three days ago.

JIM: My God! Kate! You're a trump! There's not a man in Australia good enough for you to wipe your feet on. You make me feel like a crawler.

KATE: Don't say that, Jim, I know you're not that, whatever else you may be. But you mustn't lose any time.

JIM: Look here, Kitty. You mustn't stop here, the boys are alright, but this is a rough shed, and there's one or two Cambaroora chaps in the wool-wash that might recognise you. Even if they didn't they might say something to you, and then there'd be a fight and that'd spoil all. Now I'll tell you what to do. You go up the creek a couple of miles and you'll come to an old deserted shanty. Wait there for me. I'll be there about dark and take you on to old Mother Stiffner's place on the main road. She's rough but she's a white man underneath. She'll fix you up and start you off home by the coach.

KATE: But Jim! I can take care of myself. You must—

JIM: You must do as I tell you—or I'll go and give myself up. You've done more for me than all the fine ladies I've read about in books would do for the best man in the world. I've straightened up, I've been saving money, and I meant to come back and marry you when this shed cuts out—but I'm damned if I'm going to have you mixed up in this business, and I'm damned if I'm going to have you knocking about the country like this for the sake of a blackguard like me. And I'm doubly damned if I'm going to clear out until I see you safe on the track home.

KATE: Hush, Jim, they'll hear you. As long as you get safe off I don't care.

JIM: I'm alright. You start now. But wait and I'll get you some tucker from the cook.

KATE: I've got plenty.

JIM: *(Taking roll of notes from pocket)* Here, I want you to take care of this, Kate.

KATE: But I've got money. You might want—

JIM: Take it, I say! I've got my cheque. You might want it to help me if I get caught. *(Puts notes in her hand)* Make a start now, Kate, and if I don't happen to turn up tonight, you make for old Mother Stiffner's, tell her as much as you like, and wait there a day or two for me. Then—Here come the men *(kisses her)* Get away, Kate.

(Exit Kate)

(Solus) It's Jack Drew that they'll be on the track of now. I must give him the office and start him off out of this.

(Enter the men)

JIM: Where's Macquarie?

MAN: Gone to the store for his letters—here he comes.

(Enter Jack Drew, beard etc.)

Got one for me, Macquarie?

JACK: Here you are. Here, Bogan. Here, Box-o'-Tricks. Here, Jim, there's one for you.

(Whistle blows. Shearing starts)

JIM: Hold hard, Jack. I want to speak to you. *(Brings Jack front)* We've got to smoke out of this, Jack. Cameron's knocking round here. I got the office this morning.

JACK: Damn it, that's bad, Jim.

JIM: No time to waste. The sooner we're off the better. *(Opens telegram)* "Poor Mother died last night. Heartbroken. Come home at once." *(Aside)* Kate was right.

JACK: Why, I never knew you had a mother, Jim.

JIM: That's alright. She died when I was born. This means that the traps are on our track and we've got to shift scenery pretty quick. Some chap sent this—or perhaps old Mother Stiffner. Now your horse is about the huts. Take this telegram to the boss—I'll manage without it. Your name's not Jim on the roll, but he won't notice that. Men go by all sorts of names out here. Show the wire to the boss and you'll get your cheque and get off at once.

JACK: But what about you?

JIM: I'm alright. I'll have to go up the river for my horse. There's a boss drover camped on the main road between Stiffner's shanty and the bridge. He wants men to go north and take a mob of Tyson's cattle to new country. One of the chaps told me about him this morning. I'll join him and get away in the Never-Never Country for a year or two. I'll be after you some time tonight. I'll cut across country. It would look suspicious for both of us to clear out together. Get a move on you now, Jack.

JACK: I'll see you when I get my horse.

JIM: No, the chaps will ask questions and want to give you a send-off, and that'll waste time. So-long, Jack, for the present.

JACK: So-long, Jim, and God bless you.

(Exit)

("The Shearing of the Cook's Dog" here if there's room)

(Enter Cameron)

CAMERON: I want you, Jim.

JIM: What for?

CAMERON: That horse.

JIM: But I let it go.

CAMERON: I can't help it, Jim. Here's the warrant and I've got to take you. If you can clear yourself all the better. I helped you once or twice before, Jim, and got into hot water for it. I want you to come quietly now, and I'll smooth it over with the chaps and make it as comfortable as I can for you.

JIM: I'll take my chances.

CAMERON: Then I'll have to handcuff you—that's all.

DUGGAN: What's this, Jim?

JIM: Nothing, it's alright, chaps.

Act III

SHEARER: What do you want him for, Cameron?

CAMERON: Running away from his old woman. Now are you satisfied?

DUGGAN: No we ain't. Look here, chaps, this is the squatter's work. They want to get hold of Jim for what he done in the last strike.

JIM: When I want help I'll ask for it, and I'd be damned if I'd ask a man like you to help me, Duggan.

MAN: You're right, Jim. Tell us what's the trouble and we'll send round the hat for you.

DUGGAN: But I've got an old account to settle with Mr Constable Cameron. Come on Cameron, put up your hands if you're a man.

VOICES: Go it, Duggan, we'll back you, we'll stick.

MAN: Look here, chaps, we can't have any of this sort of thing. I know Cameron, he's a white man. But if he likes to take it out of Duggan, we'll see fair play and Jim will give his word till the fight's over—won't you, Jim?

JIM: No, I'll take my chances as I've just told Cameron. Leave me out of it.

CAMERON: Come on, Jim. I don't want to handcuff you here before them all. I'll take your word anyway till we get away from the shed.

JIM: Alright.

DUGGAN: Cameron won't take off his coat because he's got his uniform on. It's a good protection for a white liver.

BOGAN: Look here! He took that coat arf wanst to save my worthless carcass whin I was drawnin' in a flood in the Lachlan, an' not wan in fifty that there was there dared face the current. And Oi'll stand by ye now, Cameron. Oi'll even fight ye meself Duggan, though ye are a bullock.

DUGGAN: Put up a man to fight for him! A mongrel Scotsman is only fit to be a trap.

JIM: I'll give you my word, Cameron, till the fight's over

and you're alright, whichever way it goes.

(Duggan and Cameron fight. Cameron wins, a collection is taken up for Jim)

CAMERON: Come on, Jim, I don't want to handcuff you here before this crowd. Give me your word to come quietly like a sensible man.

JIM: *(Aside)* Jack Drew has got clear away. *(To Cameron)* Look here, Cameron, I'd never raise a hand against you and you know it. I'll go quietly as far as the first gate, and after that I warn you, I'll take every chance I can get.

Scene II

A bush track by the river. Cameron and Jim on horseback; or Cameron on horseback and Jim handcuffed to stirrup; or both on foot having left horses tied up; or as arranged for stage.

CAMERON: Look here, Jim, don't be a damned fool! I don't want to take you twenty miles like a dog. The river is up and we must cross. I can't take you across handicapped like this. Do you want me to risk my life as well as yours in a current like the one that's running now? Make a bargain, give me your word.

JIM: I told you I'd take my chances. Make a bargain, and me handcuffed and you armed! It's time enough to talk about bargains when it's a case of man to man.

CAMERON: *(Snatching off Jim's handcuffs and throwing away his carbines)* Now it's man to man! Look here, Jim Poynton, we were boys together and mates together before you went wrong, but it's only that I know you are a white man at the bottom or I would make no difference between you and the meanest sneak thief I was ever sent to take. I've helped you out of holes more than once before today. The last time I got into hot water over it, and except for Mullaney I'd have been kicked out of the force months ago. As it is I got transferred out to this God-forsaken hole. I've got a young wife to think of now—before friendship or anything else. And now, because I'm a soft-hearted fool of a policeman, trying like a damned fool to do my duty to man and law at the same time, you of all the men in the world must try your best to baulk and humiliate me. Duty or no duty, mateship or no mateship, will you give me your word to come quietly like a sensible man, or will you fight it out here, man to man?

JIM: No, Cameron, I won't lift a hand against you. Here, take my hand and my word goes with it.

CAMERON: That's all I want, Jim *(shaking hands)*. And if anything I can do or say when we reach Cambaroora will help you in this trouble, you can count me in.

JIM: I know I can. Will you send word back to Stiffner's Shanty that I am taken?

CAMERON: I will, Jim.

JIM: Then I'm ready to cross the river.

(Exit Cameron and Jim)

Act III

Scene III

The Barwon River in flood. Enter Constable Cameron and Jim Poynton on horseback

CAMERON: It looks bad, we'll try higher up. I'll go first and you follow. My horse is used to it.

(Goes up and down over bank to right, followed by Jim. Cameron goes down into the stream, Jim remains in sight, or partly in sight of audience)

JIM: Look out, Cameron! Keep upstream!

CAMERON: Keep back, Jim! Keep back! It's too strong!

JIM: Come back, you fool! Come out!

CAMERON: I'm in a hole.

JIM: Make for the backwater! Let the horse go! Hold on to the snag! Hold on for your life!

CAMERON: Help! Jim! I'm hurt!

JIM: Don't let go. Hang on to the stump, Cameron. I'm coming!

(Forces his horse into the stream out of sight. Enter Jim carrying Cameron, who is exhausted and has a cut in his head. Jim lays Cameron down in shade of tree or bushes)

JIM: Brace up, old man, where's your Bible? *(Feels inside Cameron's coat and takes whisky flask from his pocket)* Here, try this. That's better.

CAMERON: *(Sitting up)* I'm alright; bumped my head, that's all. You saved my life, Jim, and—

JIM: *(Binding Cameron's head with handkerchief)* Nonsense, old man—

CAMERON: Clear out, Jim. I'm stunned and don't know anything. Clear out, old man, before I return to consciousness.

JIM: I'm damned if I'll leave you here like this. The rain's coming and the river rising. We must get out of the road of the water. There's an old hut in the next gully. Come on, I'll help you there for the present.

CAMERON: Jim, why didn't you join the mounted police years ago, when I wanted you to?

JIM: If there'd been more men like you in the force I might have joined.

CAMERON: If there were more scamps in the world like you, Jim, we wouldn't want a police force.

JIM: *(Helping Cameron to his feet)* Brace up, old man, here comes the water, that's alright.

(Cameron glances upriver and suddenly drops on his knees, pulling Jim down)

CAMERON: Clear out, Jim. There's some horsemen coming down the river. I just caught sight of one of them. It's the sergeant from —— I think. See, my horse got out safe down the bank. Run low and get him and make off through the timbers. Go, or by God I'll shoot you the next time I set eyes on you.

(They shake hands. Exit Jim. Enter Mullaney and troopers)

MULLANEY: Cameron! Are ye dead, me boy?

CAMERON: No, I'm all right.

MULLANEY: Where's ye're prisoner?

CAMERON: Drowned.

MULLANEY: God rest his soul. *(They take their hats off)*

Act III

Scene IV

Small office, table, chair, safe, Sawkins and Brown.

BROWN: I'm off tonight. I've come up for my share of the stuff. The best thing you can do is to take my tip and clear out too. It's madness to stop here—it was a fool's trick to come here. Jack Drew got clear off, and we might be recognised at any moment.

SAWKINS: Why, what's in the wind now? You seem to be in an infernal funk.

BROWN: You'll be in a worse one when I tell you. You've made a fool of the business. Do you remember that new revolver of mine at Cambaroora? You did a damned clever thing when you put me up to swear it belonged to Jack Drew.

SAWKINS: How's that?

BROWN: How's that? Why the gunsmith I dealt off struck my up in the street today and thanked me for putting custom in his way. He offered to make a present of a case of cartridges. That's how it is.

SAWKINS: What?

BROWN: Yes, what? He said some man came into his shop and asked for a revolver of the same pattern as the one he sent to Mr Brown, the bank manager at Cambaroora, and the gunsmith looked up his books and sold him one. That revolver business wasn't necessary at all in the first place. It was your brilliant idea, and it has set the D's on our track.

SAWKINS: What track?

BROWN: Ours, you know what I mean? Now you must count up my share of that five hundred I took from the safe and gave to you to mind. You needn't say you haven't got it here because I know you have. I'm not going to risk coming here again.

SAWKINS: Why, you're mad, mad as a hatter! What money

and what safe are you raving about? I've got no money belonging to you.

BROWN: Why, you damned scoundrel! *(Rushes at Sawkins and catches him by the throat)* Oh, that's your little game, is it? Give—me—my—money—or I'll throttle you!

SAWKINS: Hands off! Hands off, you lunatic! *(Throws him off and runs to window)* There's someone at the window. *(Catches bottom of roller blind)*

BROWN: No you don't. *(Catches hold of him)* You don't get off with that trick. *(Sawkins lets blind roll up and discovers Mitchell painting sash. Brown and Sawkins rush out)*

MITCHELL: Well I never caused such a sensation since I appeared unexpectedly one morning at the window of a Young Ladies' School Dormitory. Now I'm off to start the machinery of the law in motion.

Act III

Scene V

Ruth's lodgings. Enter Ruth.

RUTH: *(Taking small alarm clock from shelf)* Half past seven! Oh it's cruel to make girls work overtime in that shop. I feel tired to death. I would give anything for a day's rest. But, while I'm able to stand I'll not touch one penny of the doctor's hundred pounds, for it is to help Jack when the time comes. I'll set that alarm at five, that will give me time to get to the factory at six. It is hard—I don't seem to sleep a moment before the alarm rings. *(Puts clock back on shelf and sees a letter)* A letter for me! Whoever can it be from? *(Looks at postmark)* A Queensland letter! *(Opens letter)* Whatever is this? A post office order for twenty pounds! Let me see the name—it's from Jack! No Jack, no! Not while you are hunted through the bush, or banished far away from God's country for my sake. That money will go with the rest to help you. *(Sitting at table and letting her head sink on her arms)* Oh Jack! Jack! I do want you so.

(Knock at the door)

RUTH: *(Wiping her eyes)* Come in.

(Enter landlady)

LANDLADY: Why, you poor little devil! You've been crying! What's the matter?

RUTH: Nothing Mrs —— I felt lonely and tired, that was all.

LANDLADY: You haven't cooked any dinner. How's that?

RUTH: I don't feel like eating. I had a cup of tea and a scone before I came in.

LANDLADY: Don't tell me any lies. Have you got any meat?

RUTH: No, I didn't buy any, really I don't want for meat lately.

LANDLADY: Don't tell me no lies. Here. *(Puts half a crown*

on table) Go out at once and buy some meat, you poor little devil, and I'll cook it. And get some eggs and bacon for your breakfast.

RUTH: But really, Mrs ——— you are very kind, but things are not so bad as that. I have money.

LANDLADY: Don't tell me no lies, and don't you ever insult me by starving yourself to pay the rent again. I don't take rent from poor little devils like you. *(Ring)* There's that lodger of mine, that Mitchell, come home again at this hour, and his tea all parched up in the oven.

(Exit Landlady)

RUTH: He's coming up—and Mary with him. Something has happened. I feel it. *(Enter Mary and Mitchell)*

This is kind of you, Mary.

MARY: Nonsense, I'm a horrid animal for not coming before. But I'm scarcely allowed to put my nose outside the door in my new place. I met Mitchell in the street, thought I'd risk it and run in and see how you were.

RUTH: Have you heard any news, Mitchell?

MITCHELL: I never heard any news since I was born, but I got a letter for you that was at the old lodgings. *(Gives letter)*

MARY: Tell her, Jack.

MITCHELL: You tell her, I'm the worst hand in the world at telling good news.

RUTH: *(looks up from letter)* This is from— *(Notices Mary and Mitchell's manner)* what is it, Mitchell? You're keeping something from me! Tell me—tell me, Mary, don't keep me in suspense!

MARY: Tell her, Jack.

MITCHELL: The bank robbers are caught—at least one is—and the gold found!

(Ruth sinks in chair. Mary runs to her side)

MARY: *(To Mitchell)* There, I told you you'd do it. Go out of the room and go to your tea.

Act III

MITCHELL: *(Aside at door)* I'm as good as married already—when a girl speaks to me like that.

MARY: *(To Ruth)* Don't, dear—don't give way like that. Here—you've dropped your letter. *(Picks it up and gives it to Ruth)* Read it. It must be good news.

RUTH: *(Reads letter)* Mary! Mitchell! This is from the German Consul. The Doctor's money has come. Ten thousand pounds. You must stay with me tonight and till you're married, Mary. Oh, my friends, I'll be able to help you all now. Kiss Mitchell for me, Mary. Don't be ashamed—for he is as true as steel, and I want him to help find Jack. Jack!—Jack! We are rich now and the world is wide! I'll speak now and clear your name, and I'll go to the bush and find you.

CURTAIN

Act Four

Scene I

On the track. Enter Mitchell with swag, water bag and billy. Drops swag, sits on it, takes a drink from water bag and lights pipe.

MITCHELL: Well, that's another mile done. This is seven hundred odd miles from Sydney, and the chaps I meet want to know if I'm going Out Back. Hot as a camp oven all day and you could roast eggs in the dust. Salt mutton and damper, and the mosquitoes begin before the flies leave off. This is far enough Out Back for me. The Nipper's a long while back at the shanty. Oh! here he is at last.

(Enter Nipper with swag)

MITCHELL: Well, Nipper—any luck at the shanty? Did you get my flour?

NIPPER: Not a blooming pipeful.

MITCHELL: How was that? Did you pitch them a proper yarn?

NIPPER: Leave me alone for that.

Michell: Did you tell 'em that you was an orphan? That your poor brother on ahead was dying of consumption? That your step-father in Sydney ran away and left the old woman and seven kids on your hands, and that you and your brother had a job on at the next station and only wanted a handful of flour to carry you on today? Did you tell him all that?

NIPPER: No.

MITCHELL: Well, why didn't you? There's nothing like telling the truth when you're in trouble.

NIPPER: That pitch is worked out.

MITCHELL: Well—what did you tell him?

NIPPER: I didn't tell him nothing.

MITCHELL: Why?

NIPPER: 'Cos it wasn't a him. At least it wore a dress. It had a face like a ——- It was the hardest faced ole woman I ever seed, and I seed some hard 'uns. She nearly frightened me—just as if I was a kid.

MITCHELL: That's the way of it. A woman is always sure to turn up just when you don't bargain for her. It's best to always reckon with a woman in the case, when you're working an oracle—even though there mightn't be a shirt for a thousand miles. What was her politics, Nipper?

NIPPER: She didn't say much.

MITCHELL: But she got there just the same.

NIPPER: She said she'd given everything she had in the house to sundowners and loafers. She tried to borrow some flour for herself from a surveyor's camp further on but they had none to spare. She said I'd best make back to God's country, or drown myself in the first waterhole that was deep enough. She said she ought to take and knock me on the head with an axe—while I was young an' innercent—and berry me before I went further Out Back.

MITCHELL: And what did you say?

NIPPER: I didn't stop to argey with her. She's boozed or got rats.

MITCHELL: No she ain't. She's an intelligent woman, it seems to me, and her heart's in the right place. Come on and we'll work that surveyor's camp for all its worth. Here comes a colonial experienced man, or something. Get out your borrowing pipe, Nipper.

(Enter Colonial Experienced Man)
Good-day, mate.

COLONIAL EXPERIENCED MAN: Good-day.

MITCHELL: It's hot.

COLONIAL EXPERIENCED MAN: Ya-s-s. It is.

MITCHELL: Lend us a pipe of tobacco. *(C.E.M. hands out fig of tobacco)*

COLONIAL EXPERIENCED MAN: *(Aside)* What pipes!

(Mitchell talks glibly, politics, the drought—any nonsense—till he gets the new chum—who only says "Dare say", "Yes", and "No"—thoroughly confused. Mitchell hands tobacco in turn to the Nipper who cuts a pipeful.)

MITCHELL: Thanks, I suppose you keep a good supply of tobacco at the station?

COLONIAL EXPERIENCED MAN: Yass.

MITCHELL: Same brand as this?

COLONIAL EXPERIENCED MAN: Yaas—mostly, I dunno.

MITCHELL: Is your pipe full?

COLONIAL EXPERIENCED MAN: Yass, thanks, if it wasn't I would fill it.

MITCHELL: Then I'll put this piece in my pocket if you don't mind. I s'pose you find it dull here?

COLONIAL EXPERIENCED MAN: Yass, pretty dull.

MITCHELL: No one to talk to much?

COLONIAL EXPERIENCED MAN: No, not many.

MITCHELL: Tongue gets rusty?

COLONIAL EXPERIENCED MAN: Ya-as, sometimes.

MITCHELL: Well, so-long and thank you.

COLONIAL EXPERIENCED MAN: Good-day.

MITCHELL: Well, good-day, I'll see you again.

(Exit Mitchell and Nipper)

COLONIAL EXPERIENCED MAN: Well, I'm damned, blasted colonial cheek!

(Exit)

Scene II

Surveyor's camp on the track. Tents show to the right, bush to the left. Fire, kerosene tin and billies on. Some "washing" on bush—skirt and hood. Pinter mixing flour for bread in dish.

PINTER: *(Putting baking powder in flour)* There! There's enough dynamite to rise it, I reckon. I wish I had enough fat to make the pan siss, an' I'd treat meself to a fritter, but it took all the fat for them there doughboys. *(Stirs the flour round in the dish)* And this is the end of old Pinter of Ballarat. A jumped-up old slushy for a gang of lar-di-do surveyors. But it won't be much longer, as soon as I make a tidy cheque I'm off to West Australia. Ole Pinter might make his pile yet. *(Rises stiffly and puts his hand to his side)* The old pain is at it again— it'll fetch me yet. I don't seem to be getting no younger since Jim was drowned. I'm beginning to feel as if the only claim I'll ever be in again will be six foot deep, timbered with a coffin made out of gin cases an' a piano-fingered parson sayin' ashes ter ashes, dust ter dust, Pinter, an' in hopes of a great an' glorious resurrection.

(Enter Mitchell and the Nipper)

MITCHELL: We'll camp here. Drop your swag over there.

(They put down swags under sapling to right)

No one at home and a dish of flour left for us. They must have expected us. Give us the flour bag and I'll work an oracle.

(Nipper brings bag and holds it while Mitchell slips flour out of dish into bag. Nipper takes bag to swags. Mitchell wipes dish out carefully with cloth and puts it down)

Now see how that'll work. I reckon that cook thinks he got the flour out before he started. Here he comes! It's an old cove with a list to starboard. We're all right now, Nipper, because whatever complaint he's got, I'll tell him that my old man suffered from it for years, and that'll make a bond of sympathy between us.

(Enter Pinter with can of water)

PINTER: Good-day, mate!

MITCHELL: Good-day, mate!

PINTER: *(Setting can down and staring at empty dish)* What the ——- Well that settles it.

MITCHELL: Settles what? What's the trouble?

PINTER: Blest if I didn't think I got that there flour out before I went for the water.

MITCHELL: What flour?

PINTER: The flour for the bread—I could 'a' sworn I got it out in the dish and put the baking powder in.

MITCHELL: That's queer, it must be the sun. But I've done the same thing myself. It's wonderful what tricks your memory plays on you. It must be the hot weather that makes us all a bit potty.

PINTER: *(Staring at Jim)* Why! If you ain't Mitchell the painter at Cambaroora.

MITCHELL: And if you ain't old Pinter! *(They shake hands)*

PINTER: Mitchell, you must excuse me, I've been a bit queer ever since my son Jim was drowned. Tell me straight, do you know something about that flour?

MITCHELL: Pinter, I'll tell you straight and write it down if you like, and put my Colonial mark to it and take my Colonial oath on it. I *do* know something about that flour!

PINTER: Bless you, Mitchell, you've took a load off my mind. I thought I'd got rats when I seed that there dish. Is that your mate?

MITCHELL: He is. He's a cove that goes by the name of Nipper. Come here, Nipper. *(Introduces them)*

NIPPER: Glad to meet yer, old feller. Have yer got a chew of terbacco on yer?

PINTER: *(To front)* Good Lord! The old school *is* dying out—an' this is the new.

Act IV

MITCHELL: Yes, Pinter, this is the new—edited and revised up to date! We're educated in hard schools nowadays, Pinter. But I reckon our hearts are in just about the same places as the old school hearts were.

PINTER: Mebbe, and what's the news all this time?

MITCHELL: I'll never have any news till I'm a ghost. Have you heard o' Jack Drew?

PINTER: Never a word since Jim died. Poor Jack, his bones might be bleaching way out on the Never-Never now, an' I was an old mate o' his father's.

MITCHELL: You might 'a' been on old mate of my father's, Pinter—for I never heard of him.

PINTER: Mebbe. By the way, don't you ever say yer seen anything o' Pinter, in case my old woman gits on the track.

MITCHELL: I heard you ran away. Well, she was a tartar, Pinter, and I don't blame you. I see you've got some of her there. *(Pointing to dress and hood on the bush)*

PINTER: Yes, them there's her dress an' hood. Thought they'd come in handy for patchin'. Besides, her other frock was in the wash when I cut and run, 'cos I thought if I took 'em it would give me a start.

PINTER: An' what's come of 'em all at Cambaroora?

MITCHELL: Doc Lebinski died about a year ago.

PINTER: I heerd o' that. Well—hashes ter hashes—

MITCHELL: And dust to eyes. He left Miss Wilson all his money.

PINTER: Did he?

MITCHELL: And Brown was arrested, and Sawkins got clear off, and Brown confessed and died in the gaol hospital.

PINTER: I heard o' that—the infernal villains!

MITCHELL: And Mary—you remember Mary? She's companion to Miss Wilson now. Miss Wilson's been hunting for Jack ever since Brown was caught. She's been in Queensland and South Australia and Western Australia, and she'll go to the South Pole but she'll find him—dead or alive. She's that kind of a girl.

PINTER: And she'll never find him. The Dry Plains has got him long afore now. No man 'ud get lost all this time, if he was alive, with a girl like that waitin' for him. An' what are you doin' now, Mitchell?

MITCHELL: Me—Oh, I'm only a cove named Mitchell; a swaggy.

(Pinter gives Mitchell a billy of tea and a couple of pint pots, sugar, bread, meat, etc. Mitchell and Nipper sit on their swags, eat and drink. Swags and other props; positions, etc. to be arranged by Author)

PINTER: I suppose you'll go back and settle down and get married some day, Mitchell?

MITCHELL: Some day. That's it, it looks like it, doesn't it? We all say some day, I used to say it ten years ago and look at me now. I've been knocking around for over twenty years and the last one constant on the track and no show of getting off unless I go for good. I look like getting married and settling down, without a penny in my pocket or a rag to my back, scarcely, and no show of getting them. I swore I'd never go back without a cheque, and I never will—but the cheque days are past. Look at that boot. If we were down amongst the settled districts we'd be called tramps and beggars—and what's the difference? I've been a fool, but I've paid for it, and now there's nothing for it but to tramp, tramp, tramp, for graft or tucker, and keep on tramping till you get old and careless and dirty, and older and more careless, dirtier, and you get used to the heat and dust and flies and mosquitoes just as a bullock does, and lose ambition and hope and get contented with this animal life like a dog—till your swag seems part of yourself and you'd be lost and uneasy and light-shouldered without it—and you don't care a damn if you'll ever go to work again, or live like a Christian. And the spirit of a bullock takes the place of the heart of a man. Who cares? If me and the Nipper hadn't found the track yesterday when we got lost in the lignum scrub, we might have rotted there and no one been any the wiser or sorrier. Somebody might have found us in the end, but it mightn't have been worth his while to go out of his way and report us.

(Mitchell prepares to turn in. Surveyors, travellers, etc. drop into camp. "Good-day, mate. It's hot," etc.)

MITCHELL: What's the news?

SURVEYOR: The bush fires are all along the western boundary. Thousands of acres of grass and Lord knows how many miles of fencing lost. Two drovers are out on the plain knocked up.

ALL: Lost? Who are they?

SURVEYOR: I don't know. I'm going to ride back to the shanty after tea and find out how the search parties got on. We can't do any good. There's three or four parties out with good men at the head of them. Constable Cameron, Crowbar and Saltbush Bill. The men are overland drovers. They struck across country over a week ago, depending on the Ninety Mile Tank for water. They must have been mad—that tank's been dry for weeks.

(Mitchell has turned in and rolled his blanket out; also the Nipper)

SURVEYOR: Got a song, mate?

MITCHELL: I'll try.

(Mitchell, on his back, sings a song with a chorus, men join in)

ALL: Good enough! Hear! Hear! Send round the hat, Pinter.

(Pinter puts money in his hat, sends it round, and puts it down alongside Mitchell)

MITCHELL: Well, I don't know about this, mates. What do you say, Nipper?

NIPPER: Take all you can git for nothing and thanks all the same.

SURVEYOR: Here comes the coach driver, riding one horse and leading the others. He's had a break-down.

(Enter coach driver—riding one horse in harness and leading the others)

MAN: What's up, Bill? Have you drunk the coach?

DRIVER: Had a break-down about a mile back. There's two ladies coming on. Here they are. I'm going out to the shanty to send back a buggy for them. Make them comfortable.

SURVEYOR: We'll do our best. Start a man back on horseback with a tin of preserved milk and whatever else he can lay his hands on. We've got nothing here for ladies.

DRIVER: Right you are.

(Exit with horses)

SURVEYOR: Turn out of that tent, boys, and tidy up. Ladies coming. Open a couple tins of salmon and fill a bucket and a billy of water.

(Pinter seizes dress and hood and clears out)

SURVEYOR: Where are you off to, Pinter? What the devil! The old man's gone mad. He's going through the scrub like a kangaroo! Here, fetch him back, some of you chaps.

MITCHELL: It's alright, boss. It's just struck Pinter that one of those ladies might be his old woman. Turn out, Nipper, ladies coming.

SURVEYOR: Oh, the cook he married at Cambaroora. *(Men laugh)* Hush—here they are.

(Enter Ruth and Mary, dusty and tired)

SURVEYOR: Good evening, ladies. I—I'm very glad the coach broke down here. No—I mean, I'm very sorry. The fact is I want you to make yourselves at home till the buggy comes. That tent is entirely at your disposal, and if you want anything you've only got to ask for it.

RUTH: Thank you. You are very kind.

SURVEYOR: Not at all, perhaps you'd like to rest now. You won't be disturbed in the tent *(Aside to the men)* I'll do for some of you grinning fools afterwards.

RUTH: Thank you, I am tired.

(He shows her toward tent. Mary catches sight of Mitchell who has been standing staring)

MARY: Jack!

MITCHELL: Mary!

(Boss and men make signs to each other and exit hurriedly)

RUTH: Oh, Mitchell! Why didn't you write? Have you heard anything of Jack?

MITCHELL: No, never a sign. I didn't write because I had no news to tell.

RUTH: And what are you doing? Carrying your swag, you foolish fellow! Why didn't you let me know you were hard up?

MARY: And what did you mean by writing and telling me you were a road surveyor and that you'd come back as soon as you made a cheque?

MITCHELL: Well, I am a road surveyor. I've surveyed four or five hundred miles of roads since I saw you, Mary. *(Aside)* And long dusty roads they were too.

But what on earth brings you and Miss Wilson to this God-forsaken part of the country?

RUTH: I heard something in Queensland that made me think that Jack was droving south with a mob of chaps. And this is the first civilized place on the Stock Route where I'd be likely to hear of him.

MITCHELL: Well, I hope its true. This is civilized, I suppose, compared to some places. But it's no place for women.

RUTH: I'd go right across the Never-Never country if I thought I would find him. I'll never rest until I do.

MITCHELL: You must rest now, Miss Wilson, or you'll be ill. Take here to the tent, Mary.

(Mary and Ruth go into tent)

This is a bad job. Poor Jack would have heard the news or seen the advertisements in the papers and turned up long before this if he was close. It's the drought has got him for sure. And this girl will hunt for him till she's a grey-headed old woman, and his bones are crumbled to dust in the Never-Never land. Love of a girl and love of a man! There's nothing new under the sun.

(Enter Surveyor, etc.)

SURVEYOR: Are the ladies alright?

MITCHELL: Yes.

SURVEYOR: Look here, mate, they seem to know you. Now, we're a rough lot, and we've been out in this God-forgotten country so long that we've forgotten how to talk to ladies. I almost wish they hadn't come for their friend—sweet faces set a man thinking of all he's lost and make his life seem doubly a hell. Now these girls must be in some trouble or they wouldn't be out here. I want you to find out if we can help them in any way. And look here, if they're hard up *(puts hand in pocket)* that's easily fixed provided you can manage it delicately—

MAN: Hold on, boss, that's not fair—send round the hat. *(He puts a note in his hat and starts it round)*

MITCHELL: Hold on, they're not hard up.

SURVEYOR: Well, that's all we want to know. Here, you take this, and see those girls alright to wherever they're going.

MITCHELL: Thank you, mates, but I—

SURVEYOR: Don't be a fool. You need money when you're looking after ladies *(forces money on him)* The men never take it back when they send round the hat.

MITCHELL: But the girls might be only my sisters.

SURVEYOR: I wish one of 'em was.

MITCHELL: But how do you know who I am—I might be a—

SURVEYOR: Oh, you're straight or you wouldn't know girls like that.

Act IV

MITCHELL: Why, here comes an old woman. Blest if it ain't that old fool Pinter in disguise! He must have got a scare.

(Enter Pinter in dress and hood)

MAN: What the ——

SURVEYOR: Hush, don't swear.

PINTER: *(To Mitchell)* It wasn't my old woman, was it?

MITCHELL: No.

SURVEYOR: What the deuce is the meaning of all this rig, you old ass?

PINTER: Well, we're a rough looking lot, an' I thought the ladies would feel more comfortable if they saw an old woman pokin' round about the camp.

MITCHELL: Better get away, Pinter. They wouldn't feel comfortable if they saw an old woman with a monkey shave.

PINTER: Why, dang me! I clean forgot my beard. You must excuse me, I've been a bit nutty ever since my son Jim was drowned.

Here's a woman on horseback—riding like mad. It's Kate Kennedy from —— What's up now?

(Enter Kate on horseback) 'Ullo, Kate! What's the trouble?

KATE: Those two men are lost. Some of the search party came in about an hour ago. They found one of the packhorses dying, and a message written on a leaf of a pocket book. One of the men is blind with the sandy blight, and the other is sick. They were making south-west in search of water. The party picked up their tracks and followed them to about ten miles west of the out-station—then the tracks turned west and the search party had to come in for more water.

SURVEYOR: Round up your horses, you chaps. We must go out. Those men are off the track altogether. They must have lost their heads. They're dead men if they're not run down tomorrow. *(Exit men)*

PINTER: Do they know who the men are, Kate?

KATE: Yes, one goes by the name of Jim Moonlight.

PINTER: What? My God! That was Jim's shed name! My son Jim's still alive! *(Kate reels in the saddle but recovers herself as Mitchell steps to the horse's side)*

KATE: I'm alright, thanks. I felt dizzy for a moment. There's no time to lose. We want all the men we can get and all the water bags you can spare. They'll strike Dry Creek, and it's Dead Man's Track whichever way they follow it. I'll ride straight out.

(Enter Ruth from tent)

RUTH: What was the other man's name?

KATE: Macquarie Jack.

RUTH: Jack! It is Jack! That was the name he used in Queensland.

(Enter buggy and men with horses)

Oh, save them! Save them! I'll give a thousand pounds to the man that finds them.

SURVEYOR: You don't know what you're saying, Miss. Two men are lost in the scrub and likely to die of thirst—and that's all *we* need to know. If a man is lost in the bush and it is in the power of man to save him, bushmen will do it. We are all mates in the bush.

RUTH: God bless you all, for you are brave, true men.

(Ruth and Mary being assisted into the buggy. Men saddling up and mounting)

Act IV

Scene III

The edge of the plains. Night. Enter Cameron with bushmen—search party.

BUSHMAN: It's madness, Cameron! Wait till the men come up with water. We're all knocked up.

CAMERON: No, I'll go on. That smoke we saw was not from a bush fire. The lost men have had the sense to make smoke with green boughs. They can't be above ten miles. It's madness for us to go on together. Give me all the water you can spare. Take the horse back and hurry on the fresh men.

(They bring water bags which Cameron carries or slings about him)

Now get back with the horses while you can, and if there's any news make a big smoke on the sandhills for me.

BUSHMAN: All right, Cameron. But if you make a blunder and lose your tracks you're a dead man.

CAMERON: I know the country. If one of those men is the man I think he is. I've got a warrant out against him for saving my life, and by the Lord, I'll bring him in or die with him!

(Exit)

Scene IV

The Great Plains. Dazzling heat. Timber showing in the distance to the left. Dry tank in foreground. Enter Jack Drew and Jim Poynton. Jim staggering. Jack supporting him. Jack with eyes bandaged.

JIM: *(Looking into tank)* Dry! Dry as a bone! The water's been gone for days. By God, we're doomed men.

JACK: Nonsense, Jim! You're off your head a bit. Here, *(holding water bag in his mouth)* drink this.

JIM: The last drop? No.

JACK: That might carry one man through. Leave me here. *(sinking down)* I'm—I'm nearly done, Jim. I'm blind and cannot go on alone. You go on. Make for the track of that thunderstorm that passed last night. South—sou—south-east. Remember? The only chance. If you get water—make back. I've got—the—sun on my head.

JIM: *(Kneeling and supporting Jack)* God! his head is going at last. Jack, old man, for God's sake brace up! You've held me on the horse for days, you've half-carried me ever since the horses knocked up, and if you break down now it's death for us both, for I can't carry you and I won't leave you.

JACK: *(Passing his hand over his head)* This is how men live and toil and die in Australia. Aye! and women too! Through blazing heat, through sand and dust and flies—months and years—over the roofs of hell! A thousand miles over the roofs of hell! Aye! and down through the roofs of hell—for the great fame of Wool, Tallow and Hides. For the wool king's trip's to Europe. For the money to pay his wife's dress-maker in Paris. These are the things we fight through hell and die for. A wasted life! Dry bones of drovers bleaching on the sand waste to keep up a fashionable establishment in the east end of London!

Act IV

JIM: Here. *(Forces him to drink)* You're only knocked up and a bit touched by the heat. There, lie quiet in the shade. I'll go on to the sandhills ahead and look round.

JACK: It's no use, Jim. We might be a hundred miles west of the track. Make—make—make for the track of the thunderstorm. It's your only chance.

JIM: You stay quiet—don't move a foot till I come back.

(Exit, staggering)

JACK: He won't leave me—and why should two lives be sacrificed while there is a chance for one? Sheep lost, homes lost. This is the reward of two years' toil, and privation. And what remains—even if I live? The swag and the dusty hungry tracks—and sooner or later the walls of a prison! A living death for the man and a true girl dead of a broken heart. No! She shall suffer no more through me!

(Takes revolver from shirt front)

Jim didn't know I had this or he wouldn't have left me. I'll finish it now—better for Ruth, for my mate and me.

(Takes pocket knife and scratches on quart pot) "Jim, old man. You will understand. Good-bye and forgive me. If you ever get through, find means of telling her that I died in the north, long ago. That I died easy." He will understand.

(Points revolver at heart) Oh, Doctor I remember my oath to you and the time has come for its fulfilment. Intercede for me. Ruth—my girl—

(Hides revolver hurriedly in shirt front as Jim re-enters)

JIM: *(Aside, putting hand to head)* I can hold up no longer. There is nothing but sand, lignum, and the bush fire's cut us off from the east and the south. We're lost men!

(Goes to Jack. Looks down at quart pot, etc. Drops on knee by Jack's side and catches his arm, and looks in his face. Draws Jack's hand, holding revolver, from his shirt front) Jack! Would you desert your mate like this?

JACK: It would have been better, Jim. You could have

followed.

JIM: *(Aside)* I know what it's like to die of thirst—to linger in agony for days—to be driven mad with the torment—to be eaten alive by the flies and ants. My God! To have our eyes picked out by the cursed crows before we're dead! Better have done with it before the hell commences.

(Takes revolver from his pocket) There is no hope, Jack! I'll come too. *(They clasp hands)*

JACK: We'll lie together, old mate, and God forgive us!

JIM: He sees men die of thirst in the bush.

JACK: I know how they die.

JIM: Let's get it over, Jack. For Christ's sake!

JACK: Jim! I hear horse's feet.

JIM: The first sign! We'll hear running water next. Get it over, Jack—my brain's going!

JACK: I hear it now! *(Staggers to his feet)* Can you stand, Jim? We'll—we'll face Death standing.

(Jim struggles to his feet) Put my revolver to my heart—and yours to mine. Higher—there.

(Each guides and fixes muzzle of revolver with best hand)
Steady, Jim, for God's sake! Are you steady?

JIM: Yes.

JACK: Can you hold so?

JIM: Yes.

JACK: Then give me your left hand, I'll give the word. If one lives he must finish the work of both.

JIM: Shall we pray?

JACK: No—Heaven will judge.

JIM: Amen.

JACK: Are you ready, Jim?

JIM: Ready. Good-bye, old mate!

JACK: Not good-bye. Ruth—God bless her!

JIM: Kate, God bless her!

JACK: At the word three. One—

Act IV

VOICE: Stop!

JACK: Heaven forbid it.

(Drops revolver and falls on his knees as Kate Kennedy enters on horseback. Jim staggers to horse's side, puts up his arms and rests his head against pommel—or Kate's knee. She holds him so, while Cameron rushes on and kneels by Jack, supporting him.)

Who is it? Jim?

CAMERON: No—it's Cameron. Brace up, old man, you are saved.

JACK: Saved! Cameron! Why didn't you let me escape?

CAMERON: Escape? You fool! You are a free man. You are cleared. I thought bushmen had more faith and courage. Look *(pointing back)* here comes the rain!

(Lightning flashes above the horizon, thunder)

Scene V

Bar of the Overland Hotel. Girl or man behind bar. Bushmen, etc. Sawkins as swagman. Enter drover.

DROVER: Seen anything of my mate?

BUSHMAN: Yes, he's here. What's the trouble?

DROVER: I sent him on to sell a horse of mine to some chaps here, and I want to know how he got on.

BUSHMAN: Oh, he sold it alright.

DROVER: That's alright, where is he?

BUSHMAN: Joe! Show up, Joe. Here's yer Bill. *(Enter 2nd drover)*

2ND DROVER: 'Ello, Bill.

1ST DROVER: 'Ello, Joe, how did you get on?

2ND DROVER: Oh, alright. I sold the mare.

1ST DROVER: That's alright. How much did you get?

2ND DROVER: Seven quid, and I could 'a' got ten if I'd waited.

1ST DROVER: Oh, that's good enough.

2ND DROVER: I would 'a' got ten quid if I hadn't been a damn fool.

1ST DROVER: Well, it's no use crying. Seven quid is good enough. Did you get the cash?

2ND DROVER: Yes, but I could 'a' got ten quid.

1ST DROVER: Have you got the seven quid?

2ND DROVER: Well, Bill, I done it in. Can you lend me a couple of notes? I want to shout.

1ST DROVER: Well, Joe, you are a mug; but it serves me right, for I knew you was a damn fool. Come and have a drink. *(They breast the bar)*

BUSHMAN: Order for a song, you chaps.

(Bushman sings "The Bushman's Song" —Banjo. Applause. "Good for you, Mack!" "Good enough", etc. Enter Mullaney

behind the bar and Mitchell and the Nipper from door)

MULLANEY: Now thin! Arder in the court. There's ladies in the house an' there's to be no fightin' or swearin'. If here a one of yez indulges in the D.T.'s above a whisper, Oi'll run yez arl out.

MITCHELL: You used to run us in in the old days when you were in the force, Mullaney.

MULLANEY: And Oi'm in force now, in full force an' ye'd find the difference between the two. Ye'd find the difference between me runnin' yez in for a breach of the Queen's peace and yez out for a breach of mine.

NIPPER: Good day, boss. This rain will be good for the frogs.

MULLANEY: Phwhat!

NIPPER: For the frogs of the horses' feet, I mean.

MULLANEY: An' it's a good job ye meant it.

(Collars the Nipper and hauls him over the bar) There, thry yer hand at washin' some of those glasses. Yer sentenced till the risin' ov the court, ye young blaggard.

(Enter Pinter, excited)

PINTER: They're found! Me boy's found!

MULLANEY: Who's found? Ye owld lunatic.

PINTER: My boy. The boy that was drowned.

MULLANEY: The men that were baked Oi suppose ye mean. Those two drovers?

BUSHMAN: Hurrah! Who found them, are they alright? Tell us about it, Pinter.

PINTER: Kate Kennedy found 'em and Constable Cameron.

MAN: Good enough for Kate. Three rousers for Kitty, boys. Hip! Hip! Hooray! Three cheers for Cameron! The whitest man in the force! Hip! — etc.

(Shouts outside: "Here they are!")

(Enter Jack Drew, Jim, Kate, Cameron. Congratulations)

SAWKINS: I know that man, he's Jack Drew, an escaped prisoner—he's wanted for the bank robbery at Cambaroora.

CAMERON: And who are you?

MAN: A damned informer anyway.

CAMERON: Who are you?

SAWKINS: My name's James Brown. I am a shearer.

(Ruth enters)

RUTH: It's a lie. I know him in spite of his disguise. He is Sawkins, the real robber.

CAMERON: Sawkin? Then he's the man we want.

(Arrests Sawkins)

JACK: Ruth! Ruth! Am I going mad?

RUTH: *(Going to his arms)* No, Jack, poor boy. Your troubles are over now.

(Pinter, who has been making a general fool of himself, puts a pound note in his hat and goes round with it. Jim—Kate—Mary and Mitchell together. Pinter in front holding hat full of money in both hands and staring vacantly at it)

MITCHELL: Why, Pinter! What are you doing?

PINTER: Dang me if I haven't been a bit queer ever since I heard that my son Jim wasn't drowned.

MAN: Then take up another collection for yerself, Pinter, old man. There's plenty more where that came from.

MULLANEY: An' here's a foiver toward it. Be the luck o' things Oi think it will go for a weddin' present to the wife o' Pinter's son Jim.

CURTAIN

The Hero of Redclay
(1899)

THE "BOSS-OVER-THE-BOARD" was leaning with his back to the wall between two shoots, reading a reference handed to him by a green-hand applying for work as picker-up or woolroller—a shed rouseabout. It was terribly hot. I was slipping past to the rolling-tables, carrying three fleeces to save a journey; we were only supposed to carry two. The boss stopped me:

"You've got three fleeces there, young man?"

"Yes."

Notwithstanding the fact that I had just slipped a light ragged fleece into the belly-wool and "bits" basket, I felt deeply injured, and righteously and fiercely indignant at being pulled up. It was a fearfully hot day.

"If I catch you carrying three fleeces again," said the boss quietly, "I'll give you the sack."

"I'll take it now if you like," I said.

He nodded. "You can go on picking-up in this man's place," he said to the jackeroo, whose reference showed him to be a non-union man—a "free-labourer", as the pastoralists had it, or, in plain shed terms, "a blanky scab". He was now in the comfortable position of a non-unionist in a union shed who had jumped into a sacked man's place.

Somehow the lurid sympathy of the men irritated me worse than the boss-over-the-board had done. It must have been on account of the heat, as Mitchell says. I was sick of the shed and the life. It was within a couple of days of cut-out, so I told Mitchell—who was shearing—that I'd camp up the Billabong and wait for him; got my cheque, rolled up my swag, got three days' tucker from the cook, said so-long to him, and tramped while the men were in the shed.

I camped at the head of the Billabong where the track branched, one branch running to Bourke, up the river, and the other out towards the Paroo—and hell.

About ten o'clock the third morning Mitchell came along with his cheque and his swag, and a new sheep-pup, and his quiet grin; and I wasn't too pleased to see that he had a shearer called "the Lachlan" with him.

The Lachlan wasn't popular at the shed. He was a brooding, unsociable sort of man, and it didn't make any difference to the chaps whether he had a union ticket or not. It was pretty well known in the shed—there were three or four chaps from the district he was reared in—that he'd done five years hard for burglary. What surprised me was that Jack Mitchell seemed thick with him; often, when the Lachlan was sitting brooding and smoking by himself outside the hut after sunset, Mitchell would perch on his heels alongside him and yarn. But no one else took notice of anything Mitchell did out of the common.

"Better camp with us till the cool of the evening," said Mitchell to the Lachlan, as they slipped their swags. "Plenty time for you to start after sundown, if you're going to travel to-night."

So the Lachlan was going to travel all night and on a different track. I felt more comfortable, and put the billy on. I did not care so much what he'd been or had done, but I was green and soft yet, and his presence embarrassed me.

They talked shearing, sheds, tracks, and a little unionism—the Lachlan speaking in a quiet voice and with a lot of sound, common sense, it seemed to me. He was tall and gaunt, and might have been thirty, or even well on in the forties. His eyes were dark brown and deep set, and had something of the dead-earnest sad expression you saw in the eyes of union leaders and secretaries—the straight men of the strikes of '90 and '91. I fancied once or twice I saw in his eyes the sudden furtive look of the "bad egg" when a mounted trooper is spotted near the shed; but perhaps this was prejudice. And with it all there was about the Lachlan something of the man who has lost all he had and the chances of all he was ever likely to have, and is past feeling, or caring, or flaring up—past getting mad about anything—something, all the same, that warned men not to make free with him.

He and Mitchell fished along the Billabong all the afternoon; I fished a little, and lay about the camp and read. I had an instinct that the Lachlan saw I didn't cotton on to his camping with us, though he wasn't the sort of man to show what he saw or felt. After tea, and a smoke at sunset, he shouldered his swag, nodded to me as if I was an accidental but respectful stranger at a funeral that belonged to him, and took the outside track. Mitchell walked along the track with him for a mile or so, while I poked round and got some boughs down for a bed, and fed and studied the collie pup that Jack had bought from the shearers' cook.

I saw them stop and shake hands out on the dusty clearing, and they seemed to take a long time about it; then Mitchell started back, and the other began to dwindle down to a black peg and then to a dot on the sandy plain, that had just a hint of dusk and dreamy far-away gloaming on it between the change from glaring day to hard, bare, broad moonlight.

I thought Mitchell was sulky, or had got the blues, when he came back; he lay on his elbow smoking, with his face turned from the camp towards the plain. After a bit I got wild—if Mitchell was going to go on like that he might as well have taken his swag and gone with the Lachlan. I don't know exactly what was the matter with me that day, and at last I made up my mind to bring the thing to a head.

"You seem mighty thick with the Lachlan," I said.

"Well, what's the matter with that?" asked Mitchell. "It ain't the first felon I've been on speaking terms with. I borrowed half-a-caser off a murderer once, when I was in a hole and had no one else to go to; and the murderer hadn't served his time, neither. I've got nothing against the Lachlan, except that he's a white man and bears a faint family resemblance to a certain branch of my tribe."

I rolled out my swag on the boughs, got my pipe, tobacco, and matches handy in the crown of a spare hat, and lay down.

Mitchell got up, re-lit his pipe at the fire, and mooned round for a while, with his hands behind him, kicking sticks out of the road, looking out over the plain, down along the Billabong, and up through the mulga branches at the stars; then he comforted the pup a bit, shoved the fire together with his toe, stood the tea-billy on the coals, and came and squatted on the sand by my head.

"Joe! I'll tell you a yarn."

"All right; fire away! Has it got anything to do with the Lachlan?"

"No. It's got nothing to do with the Lachlan now; but it's about a chap he knew. Don't you ever breathe a word of this to the Lachlan or anyone, or he'll get on to me."

"All right. Go ahead."

"You know I've been a good many things in my time. I did a deal of house-painting at one time; I was a pretty smart brush hand, and made money at it. Well, I had a run of work at a place called Redclay, on the Lachlan side. You know the sort of town—two pubs, a general store, a post office, a blacksmith's shop, a police station, a branch bank, and a dozen private weatherboard boxes on piles, with galvanized-iron tops, besides the humpies. There was a paper there, too, called the *Redclay Advertiser* (with which was incorporated the *Geebung Chronicle*), and a Roman Catholic church, a Church of England, and a Wesleyan chapel. Now you see more of private life in the house-painting line than in any other—bar plumbing and gasfitting; but I'll tell you about my house-painting experiences some other time.

"There was a young chap named Jack Drew editing the *Advertiser* then. He belonged to the district, but had been sent to Sydney to a grammar school when he was a boy. He was between twenty-five and thirty; had knocked round a good deal, and gone the pace in Sydney. He got on as a boy reporter on one of the big dailies; he had brains and could write rings round a good many, but he got in with a crowd that called themselves 'Bohemians', and the drink got a hold on him. The paper stuck to him as long as it could (for the sake of his brains), but they had to sack him at last.

"He went out back, as most of them do, to try and work out their salvation, and knocked round amongst the sheds. He 'picked up' in one shed where I was shearing, and we carried swags together for a couple of months. Then he went back to the Lachlan side, and prospected amongst the old fields round there with his elder brother Tom, who was all there was left of his family. Tom, by the way, broke his heart digging Jack out of a cave in a drive they were working, and died a few minutes after the rescue. But that's another yarn. Jack Drew had a bad spree after that; then he went to Sydney again, got on his old paper, went to the dogs, and a Parliamentary push that owned some city fly-blisters and country papers sent him up to edit the *Advertiser* at two quid a week. He drank again, and no wonder—you don't know what it is to run a *Geebung Advocate* or *Mudgee Budgee Chronicle*, and live there. He was about the same build as the Lachlan, but stouter, and had something the same kind of eyes; but he was ordinarily as careless and devil-may-care as the Lachlan is grumpy and quiet.

"There was a doctor there, called Dr. Lebinski. They said he was a Polish exile. He was fifty or sixty, a tall man, with the set of an old soldier when he stood straight; but he mostly walked with his hands behind him, studying the ground. Jack Drew caught that trick off him towards the end. They were chums in a gloomy way, and kept to themselves—they were the only two men with brains in that town. They drank and fought the drink together. The Doctor was too gloomy and impatient over little things to be popular. Jack Drew talked too straight in the paper, and in spite of his proprietors—about pub spieling and such things—and was too sarcastic in his progress committee, town council, and toady reception reports. The Doctor had a hawk's nose, pointed grizzled beard and moustache, and steely-grey eyes with a haunted look in them sometimes (especially when he glanced at you sideways), as if he loathed his fellow men, and couldn't always hide it; or as if you were the spirit of morphia or opium, or a dead girl he'd wronged in his youth—or whatever his devil was, beside drink. He was clever, and drink had brought him down to Redclay.

"The bank manager was a heavy snob named Browne. He complained of being a bit dull of hearing in one ear—after you'd yelled at him three or four times; sometimes I've thought he was as deaf as a book-keeper in both. He had a wife and youngsters, but they were away on a visit while I was working in Redclay. His niece—or, rather, his wife's niece—a girl named Ruth Wilson, did the housekeeping. She was an orphan, adopted by her aunt, and was general slavey and scape-goat to the family—especially to the brats, as is often the case. She was rather pretty, and lady-like, and kept to herself. The women and girls called her Miss Wilson, and didn't like her. Most of the single men—and some of the married ones, perhaps—were gone on her, but hadn't the brains or the pluck to bear up and try their luck. I was gone worse than any, I think, but had too much experience or common sense. She was very good to me—used to hand me out cups of tea and plates of sandwiches, or bread and butter, or cake, mornings and afternoons the whole time I was painting the bank. The Doctor had known her people and was very kind to her. She was about the only woman—for she was more woman than girl—that he'd brighten up and talk for. Neither he nor Jack Drew were particularly friendly with Browne or his push.

"The banker, the storekeeper, one of the publicans, the butcher (a popular man with his hands in his pockets, his hat on the back of his head, and nothing in it), the postmaster, and his toady, the lightning squirter, were the scrub-aristocracy. The rest were crawlers, mostly pub spielers and bush larrikins, and the women were hags and larrikinesses. The town lived on cheque-men from the surrounding bush. It was a nice little place, taking it all round.

"I remember a ball at the local town hall, where the scrub aristocrats took one end of the room to dance in and the ordinary scum the other. It was a saving in music. Some day an Australian writer will come along who'll remind the critics and readers of Dickens, Carlyle, and Thackeray mixed, and he'll do justice to these little customs of ours in the little settled-district towns of Democratic Australia. This sort of thing came to a head one New Year's Night at Redclay, when there was a `public' ball and peace on earth and good will towards all men—mostly on account of a railway to Redclay being surveyed. We were all there. They'd got the Doc out of his shell to act as M.C.

"One of the aristocrats was the daughter of the local storekeeper; she belonged to the lawn-tennis clique, and they *were* select. For some reason or other—because she looked upon Miss Wilson as a slavey, or on account of a fancied slight, or the heat working on ignorance, or on account of something that comes over girls and women that no son of sin can account for—this Miss Tea-'n'-sugar tossed her head and refused Miss Wilson's hand in the first set and so broke the ladies' chain and the dance. Then there was a to-do. The Doctor held up his hand to stop the music, and said, very quietly, that he must call upon Miss So-and-so to apologise to Miss Wilson—or resign the chair. After a lot of fuss the girl did apologise in a snappy way that was another insult. Jack Drew gave Miss Wilson his arm and marched her off without a word—I saw she was almost crying. Some one said, `Oh, let's go on with the dance.' The Doctor flashed round on them, but they were too paltry for him, so he turned on his heel and went out without a word. But I was beneath them again in social standing, so there was nothing to prevent me from making a few well-chosen remarks on things in general—which I did; and broke up that ball, and broke some heads afterwards, and got myself a good deal of hatred and respect, and two sweethearts; and lost all the jobs I was likely to get, except at the bank, the Doctor's, and the Royal.

"One day it was raining—general rain for a week. Rain, rain, rain, over ridge and scrub and galvanised iron and into the dismal creeks. I'd done all my inside work, except a bit under the Doctor's verandah, where he'd been having some patching and altering done round the glass doors of his surgery, where he consulted his patients. I didn't want to lose time. It was a Monday and no day for the Royal, and there was no dust, so it was a good day for varnishing. I took a pot and brush and went along to give the Doctor's doors a coat of varnish. The Doctor and Drew were inside with a fire, drinking whisky and smoking, but I didn't know that when I started work. The rain roared on the iron roof like the sea. All of a sudden it held up for a minute, and I heard their voices. The doctor had been shouting on account of the rain, and forgot to lower his voice. 'Look here, Jack Drew,' he said, 'there are only two things for you to do if you have any regard for that girl; one is to stop this' (the liquor I suppose he meant) 'and pull yourself together; and I don't think you'll do that — I know men. The other is to throw up the *Advertiser*—it's doing you no good—and clear out.' 'I won't do that,' says Drew. 'Then shoot yourself,' said the Doctor. '(There's another flask in the cupboard). You know what this hole is like . . . She's a good true girl—a girl as God made her. I knew her father and mother, and I tell you, Jack, I'd sooner see her dead than . . .' The roof roared again. I felt a bit delicate about the business and didn't like to disturb them, so I knocked off for the day.

"About a week before that I was down in the bed of the Redclay Creek fishing for 'tailers'. I'd been getting on all right with the housemaid at the 'Royal'—she used to have plates of pudding and hot pie for me on the big gridiron arrangement over the kitchen range; and after the third tuck-out I thought it was good enough to do a bit of a bear-up in that direction. She mentioned one day, yarning, that she liked a stroll by the creek sometimes in the cool of the evening. I thought she'd be off that day, so I said I'd go for a fish after I'd knocked off. I thought I might get a bite. Anyway, I didn't catch Lizzie—tell you about that some other time.

"It was Sunday. I'd been fishing for Lizzie about an hour when I saw a skirt on the bank out of the tail of my eye—and thought I'd got a bite, sure. But I was had. It was Miss Wilson strolling along the bank in the sunset, all by her pretty self. She was a slight girl, not very tall, with reddish frizzled hair, grey eyes, and small, pretty features. She spoke as if she had more brains than the average, and had been better educated. Jack Drew was the only young man in Redclay she could talk to, or who could talk to a girl like her; and that was the whole trouble in a nutshell. The newspaper office was next to the bank, and I'd seen her hand cups of tea and cocoa over the fence to his office window more than once, and sometimes they yarned for a while.

"She said, `Good morning, Mr. Mitchell.'

"I said, `Good morning, Miss.'

"There's some girls I can't talk to like I'd talk to other girls. She asked me if I'd caught any fish, and I said, `No, Miss.' She asked me if it wasn't me down there fishing with Mr. Drew the other evening, and I said, `Yes—it was me.' Then presently she asked me straight if he was fishing down the creek that afternoon? I guessed they'd been down fishing for each other before. I said, `No, I thought he was out of town.' I knew he was pretty bad at the Royal. I asked her if she'd like to have a try with my line, but she said No, thanks, she must be going; and she went off up the creek. I reckoned Jack Drew had got a bite and landed her. I felt a bit sorry for her, too.

"The next Saturday evening after the rainy Monday at the Doctor's, I went down to fish for tailers—and Lizzie. I went down under the banks to where there was a big she-oak stump half in the water, going quietly, with an idea of not frightening the fish. I was just unwinding the line from my rod, when I noticed the end of another rod sticking out from the other side of the stump; and while I watched it was dropped into the water. Then I heard a murmur, and craned my neck round the back of the stump to see who it was. I saw the back view of Jack Drew and Miss Wilson; he had his arm round her waist, and her head was on his shoulder. She said, `I *will* trust you, Jack—I know you'll give up the drink for my sake. And I'll help you, and we'll be so happy!' or words in that direction. A thunderstorm was coming on. The sky had darkened up with a great blue-black storm-cloud rushing over, and they hadn't noticed it. I didn't mind, and the fish bit best in a storm. But just as she said 'happy' came a blinding flash and a crash that shook the ridges, and the first drops came peltering down. They jumped up and climbed the bank, while I perched on the she-oak roots over the water to be out of sight as they passed. Half way to the town I saw them standing in the shelter of an old stone chimney that stood alone. He had his overcoat round her and was sheltering her from the wind. . . ."

"Smoke-oh, Joe. The tea's stewing."

Mitchell got up, stretched himself, and brought the billy and pint-pots to the head of my camp. The moon had grown misty. The plain horizon had closed in. A couple of boughs, hanging from the gnarled and blasted timber over the billabong, were the perfect shapes of two men hanging side by side. Mitchell scratched the back of his neck and looked down at the pup curled like a glob of mud on the sand in the moonlight, and an idea struck him. He got a big old felt hat he had, lifted his pup, nose to tail, fitted it in the hat, shook it down, holding the hat by the brim, and stood the hat near the head of his doss, out of the moonlight. "He might get moonstruck," said Mitchell, "and I don't want that pup to be a genius." The pup seemed perfectly satisfied with this new arrangement.

"Have a smoke," said Mitchell. "You see," he added, with a sly grin, "I've got to make up the yarn as I go along, and it's hard work. It seems to begin to remind me of yarns your grandmother or aunt tells of things that happened when she was a girl—but those yarns are true. You won't have to listen long now; I'm well on into the second volume.

"After the storm I hurried home to the tent—I was batching with a carpenter. I changed my clothes, made a fire in the fire-bucket with shavings and ends of soft wood, boiled the billy, and had a cup of coffee. It was Saturday night. My mate was at the Royal; it was cold and dismal in the tent, and there was nothing to read, so I reckoned I might as well go up to the Royal, too, and put in the time.

"I had to pass the Bank on the way. It was the usual weatherboard box with a galvanised iron top—four rooms and a passage, and a detached kitchen and wash-house at the back; the front room to the right (behind the office) was the family bedroom, and the one opposite it was the living room. The *Advertiser* office was next door. Jack Drew camped in a skillion room behind his printing office, and had his meals at the Royal. I noticed the storm had taken a sheet of iron off the skillion, and supposed he'd sleep at the Royal that night. Next to the *Advertiser* office was the police station (still called the Police Camp) and the Courthouse. Next was the Imperial Hotel, where the scrub aristocrats went. There was a vacant allotment on the other side of the Bank, and I took a short cut across this to the Royal.

"They'd forgotten to pull down the blind of the dining-room window, and I happened to glance through and saw she had Jack Drew in there and was giving him a cup of tea. He had a bad cold, I remember, and I suppose his health had got precious to her, poor girl. As I glanced she stepped to the window and pulled down the blind, which put me out of face a bit—though, of course, she hadn't seen me. I was rather surprised at her having Jack in there, till I heard that the banker, the postmaster, the constable, and some others were making a night of it at the Imperial, as they'd been doing pretty often lately—and went on doing till there was a blow-up about it, and the constable got transferred Out Back. I used to drink my share then. We smoked and played cards and yarned and filled 'em up again at the Royal till after one in the morning. Then I started home.

"I'd finished giving the Bank a couple of coats of stone-colour that week, and was cutting in in dark colour round the spouting, doors, and window-frames that Saturday. My head was pretty clear going home, and as I passed the place it struck me that I'd left out the only varnish brush I had. I'd been using it to give the sashes a coat of varnish colour, and remembered that I'd left it on one of the window-sills—the sill of her bedroom window, as it happened. I knew I'd sleep in next day,

Sunday, and guessed it would be hot, and I didn't want the varnish tool to get spoiled; so I reckoned I'd slip in through the side gate, get it, and take it home to camp and put it in oil. The window sash was jammed, I remember, and I hadn't been able to get it up more than a couple of inches to paint the runs of the sash. The grass grew up close under the window, and I slipped in quietly. I noticed the sash was still up a couple of inches. Just as I grabbed the brush I heard low voices inside—Ruth Wilson's and Jack Drew's—in her room.

"The surprise sent about a pint of beer up into my throat in a lump. I tip-toed away out of there. Just as I got clear of the gate I saw the banker being helped home by a couple of cronies.

"I went home to the camp and turned in, but I couldn't sleep. I lay think—think—thinking, till I thought all the drink out of my head. I'd brought a bottle of ale home to last over Sunday, and I drank that. It only made matters worse. I didn't know how I felt—I—well, I felt as if I was as good a man as Jack Drew—I—you see I've—you might think it soft—but I loved that girl, not as I've been gone on other girls, but in the old-fashioned, soft, honest, hopeless, far-away sort of way; and now, to tell the straight truth, I thought I might have had her. You lose a thing through being too straight or sentimental, or not having enough cheek; and another man comes along with more brass in his blood and less sentimental rot and takes it up—and the world respects him; and you feel in your heart that you're a weaker man than he is. Why, part of the time I must have felt like a man does when a better man runs away with his wife. But I'd drunk a lot, and was upset and lonely-feeling that night.

"Oh, but Redclay had a tremendous sensation next day! Jack Drew, of all the men in the world, had been caught in the act of robbing the bank. According to Browne's account in court and in the newspapers, he returned home that night at about twelve o'clock (which I knew was a lie, for I saw him being helped home nearer two) and immediately retired to rest (on top of the quilt, boots and all, I suppose). Some time before daybreak he was roused by a fancied noise (I suppose it was his head swelling); he rose, turned up a night lamp (he hadn't lit it, I'll swear), and went through the dining-room passage and office to investigate (for whisky and water). He saw that the doors and windows were secure, returned to bed, and fell asleep again.

"There is something in a deaf person's being roused easily. I know the case of a deaf chap who'd start up at a step or movement in the house when no one else could hear or feel it; keen sense of vibration, I reckon. Well, just at daybreak (to shorten the yarn) the banker woke suddenly, he said, and heard a crack like a shot in the house. There was a loose flooring-board in the passage that went off like a pistol-shot sometimes when you trod on it; and I guess Jack Drew trod on it, sneaking out, and he weighed nearly twelve stone. If the truth were known, he probably heard Browne poking round, tried the window, found the sash jammed, and was slipping through the passage to the back door. Browne got his revolver, opened his door suddenly, and caught Drew standing between the girl's door (which was shut) and the office door, with his coat on his arm and his boots in his hands. Browne covered him with his revolver, swore he'd shoot if he moved, and yelled for help. Drew stood a moment like a man stunned; then he rushed Browne, and in the struggle the revolver went off, and Drew got hit in the arm. Two of the mounted troopers—who'd been up looking to the horses for an early start somewhere—rushed in then, and took Drew. He had nothing to say. What could he say? He couldn't say he was a blackguard who'd taken advantage of a poor unprotected girl because she loved him. They found the back door unlocked, by the way, which was put down to the burglar; of course Browne couldn't explain that he came home too muddled to lock doors after him.

"And the girl? She shrieked and fell when the row started, and they found her like a log on the floor of her room after it was over.

"They found in Jack's overcoat pocket a parcel containing a

cold chisel, small screw-wrench, file, and one or two other things that he'd bought that evening to tinker up the old printing press. I knew that, because I'd lent him a hand a few nights before, and he told me he'd have to get the tools. They found some scratches round the key-hole and knob of the office door that I'd made myself, scraping old splashes of paint off the brass and hand-plate so as to make a clean finish. Oh, it taught me the value of circumstantial evidence! If I was judge I wouldn't give a man till the `risin' av the coort' on it, any more than I would on the bare word of the noblest woman breathing.

"At the preliminary examination Jack Drew said he was guilty. But it seemed that, according to law, he couldn't be guilty until after he was committed. So he was committed for trial at the next Quarter Sessions. The excitement and gabble were worse than the Dean case, or Federation, and sickened me, for they were all on the wrong track. You lose a lot of life through being behind the scenes. But they cooled down presently to wait for the trial.

"They thought it best to take the girl away from the place where she'd got the shock; so the Doctor took her to his house, where he had an old housekeeper who was as deaf as a post—a first class recommendation for a housekeeper anywhere. He got a nurse from Sydney to attend on Ruth Wilson, and no one except he and the nurse were allowed to go near her. She lay like dead, they said, except when she had to be held down raving; brain fever, they said, brought on by the shock of the attempted burglary and pistol shot. Dr. Lebinski had another doctor up from Sydney at his own expense, but nothing could save her—and perhaps it was as well. She might have finished her life in a lunatic asylum. They were going to send her to Sydney, to a brain hospital; but she died a week before the Sessions. She was right-headed for an hour, they said, and asking all the time for Jack. The Doctor told her he was all right and was coming—and, waiting and listening for him, she died.

"The case was black enough against Drew now. I knew he

wouldn't have the pluck to tell the truth now, even if he was that sort of a man. I didn't know what to do, so I spoke to the Doctor straight. I caught him coming out of the Royal, and walked along the road with him a bit. I suppose he thought I was going to show cause why his doors ought to have another coat of varnish.

"'Hallo, Mitchell!' he said, 'how's painting?'

"'Doctor!' I said, 'what am I going to do about this business?'

"'What business?'

"'Jack Drew's.'

"He looked at me sideways—the swift haunted look. Then he walked on without a word, for half a dozen yards, hands behind, and studying the dust. Then he asked, quite quietly:

"'Do you know the truth?'

"'Yes!'

"About a dozen yards this time; then he said:

"'I'll see him in the morning, and see you afterwards,' and he shook hands and went on home.

"Next day he came to me where I was doing a job on a step ladder. He leaned his elbow against the steps for a moment, and rubbed his hand over his forehead, as if it ached and he was tired.

"'I've seen him, Mitchell,' he said.

"'Yes.'

"'You were mates with him, once, Out Back?'

"'I was.'

"'You know Drew's hand-writing?'

"'I should think so.'

"He laid a leaf from a pocketbook on top of the steps. I read the message written in pencil:

"'To Jack Mitchell—We were mates on the track. If you know anything of my affair, don't give it away—J. D.'

"I tore the leaf and dropped the bits into the paint-pot.

"'That's all right, Doctor,' I said; 'but is there no way?'

"'None.'

"He turned away, wearily. He'd knocked about so much

over the world that he was past bothering about explaining things or being surprised at anything. But he seemed to get a new idea about me; he came back to the steps again, and watched my brush for a while, as if he was thinking, in a broody sort of way, of throwing up his practice and going in for house-painting. Then he said, slowly and deliberately:

"'If she—the girl—had lived, we might have tried to fix it up quietly. That's what I was hoping for. I don't see how we can help him now, even if he'd let us. He would never have spoken, anyway. We must let it go on, and after the trial I'll go to Sydney and see what I can do at headquarters. It's too late now. You understand, Mitchell?'

"'Yes. I've thought it out.'

"Then he went away towards the Royal.

"And what could Jack Drew or we do? Study it out whatever way you like. There was only one possible chance to help him, and that was to go to the judge; and the judge that happened to be on that circuit was a man who—even if he did listen to the story and believe it—would have felt inclined to give Jack all the more for what he was charged with. Browne was out of the question. The day before the trial I went for a long walk in the bush, but couldn't hit on anything that the Doctor might have missed.

"I was in the court—I couldn't keep away. The Doctor was there too. There wasn't so much of a change in Jack as I expected, only he had the gaol white in his face already. He stood fingering the rail, as if it was the edge of a table on a platform and he was a tired and bored and sleepy chairman waiting to propose a vote of thanks."

The only well-known man in Australia who reminds me of Mitchell is Bland Holt, the comedian. Mitchell was about as good hearted as Bland Holt, too, under it all; but he was bigger and roughened by the bush. But he seemed to be taking a heavy part to-night, for, towards the end of his yarn, he got up and walked up and down the length of my bed, dropping the sentences as he turned towards me. He'd folded his arms high and tight, and his face in the moonlight was — well, it was very different from his careless tone of voice. He was like—like an actor acting tragedy and talking comedy. Mitchell went on, speaking quickly—his voice seeming to harden:

***

"The charge was read out—I forget how it went—it sounded like a long hymn being given out. Jack pleaded guilty. Then he straightened up for the first time and looked round the court, with a calm, disinterested look—as if we were all strangers and he was noting the size of the meeting. And—it's a funny world, ain't it?—everyone of us shifted or dropped his eyes, just as if we were the felons and Jack the judge. Everyone except the Doctor; he looked at Jack and Jack looked at him. Then the Doctor smiled—I can't describe it—and Drew smiled back. It struck me afterwards that I should have been in that smile. Then the Doctor did what looked like a strange thing—stood like a soldier with his hands to Attention. I'd noticed that, whenever he'd made up his mind to do a thing, he dropped his hands to his sides: it was a sign that he couldn't be moved. Now he slowly lifted his hand to his forehead, palm out, saluted the prisoner, turned on his heel, and marched from the court-room. `He's boozin' again,' someone whispered. `He's got a touch of 'em.' `My oath, he's ratty!' said someone else. One of the traps said:

"`Arder in the car-rt!'

"The judge gave it to Drew red-hot on account of the burglary being the cause of the girl's death and the sorrow in a respectable family; then he gave him five years' hard.

"It gave me a lot of confidence in myself to see the law of the land barking up the wrong tree, while only I and the Doctor and the prisoner knew it. But I've found out since then that the law is often the only one that knows it's barking up the wrong tree."

***

Mitchell prepared to turn in.

"And what about Drew," I asked.

"Oh, he did his time, or most of it. The Doctor went to headquarters, but either a drunken doctor from a geebung town wasn't of much account, or they weren't taking any romance just then at headquarters. So the Doctor came back, drank heavily, and one frosty morning they found him on his back on the bank of the creek, with his face like note-paper where the blood hadn't dried on it, and an old pistol in his hand—that he'd used, they said, to shoot Cossacks from horseback when he was a young dude fighting in the bush in Poland."

Mitchell lay silent a good while; then he yawned.

"Ah, well! It's a lonely track the Lachlan's tramping to-night; but I s'pose he's got his ghosts with him."

I'd been puzzling for the last half-hour to think where I'd met or heard of Jack Drew; now it flashed on me that I'd been told that Jack Drew was the Lachlan's real name.

I lay awake thinking a long time, and wished Mitchell had kept his yarn for daytime. I felt—well, I felt as if the Lachlan's story should have been played in the biggest theatre in the world, by the greatest actors, with music for the intervals and situations—deep, strong music, such as thrills and lifts a man from his boot soles. And when I got to sleep I hadn't slept a moment, it seemed to me, when I started wide awake to see those infernal hanging boughs with a sort of nightmare idea that the Lachlan hadn't gone, or had come back, and he and Mitchell had hanged themselves sociably—Mitchell for sympathy and the sake of mateship.

But Mitchell was sleeping peacefully, in spite of a path of moonlight across his face—and so was the pup.

www.ingramcontent.com/pod-product-compliance
Lightning Source LLC
Chambersburg PA
CBHW022018290426
44109CB00015B/1217